CONFESSIONS OF A HOLLYWOOD PUBLICIST

This book is dedicated by the Author in memory of James Willet Freemans and William F. Fischer.

Dan Meyers

12/15/03

CONFESSIONS OF A HOLLYWOOD PUBLICIST

Revelations on HOW PUBLICISTS CREATE STAR POWER…and what happens behind the scenes everywhere from Los Angeles to New York to Kansas City…from Clint Eastwood, Steven Seagal, and Halle Berry to Stanley Kubrick, George Burns, and Rush Limbaugh

Daniel D. Meyers, APR

Four-Star Press

12/03

★★★★
FOUR-STAR PRESS
One Orion Place
P. O. Box 5825
Kansas City, MO 64171-0825

Manufactured in the United States of America

First Edition 10 9 8 7 6 5 4 3 2 1

Library of Congress Control Number 2001118799

ISBN 0-9710587-0-9
ISBN 0-9710587-1-7 (Collectors Edition)

The Collectors Edition is limited to 500 signed and numbered copies.

gift

CONTENTS

Introduction

Confessions of a Hollywood Publicist travels through time between the Hollywoods in Los Angeles, New York, Kansas City, and cities and towns everywhere. I first take you back to the golden age of the movies and then forward into today's digital era.

I share with you, for the first time, my own unconventional definition of "Hollywood."

There have been Hollywood publicists in all the major cities since the early heyday of the studios. In fact, when I began as a movie publicist in the 1960's, most publicity and advertising personnel were located in New York, not at the studios in Los Angeles.

My career began near the end of the old Hollywood system when a publicist was an employee, directly responsible to studio bosses. As an independent publicist for Warner Bros., I was compensated on a fee basis.

Our office handled Warner Bros. publicity, promotion, public relations, and advertising in four-states: Missouri, Kansas, Iowa, and Nebraska.

The formation of my own organization, Dan Meyers and Company, allowed me to be an agent, initially, for several major studios, including Tri-Star, Universal, 20th Century Fox, United Artists, MGM, Disney, and Paramount.

The showmanship stories in this book are intended to entertain and instruct the general reader. However, the ideas can be applied to the fields of business and education for courses in film studies, public relations, communications, and direct marketing.

I hope you enjoy reading this book as much as my wife, Ruby, and I have enjoyed living it.

Daniel D. Meyers, APR

Tibbetts '97

ONE

How I Found The True Hollywood:
An Insider's Unconventional View

Hollywood—a place where people from Iowa mistake each other for movie stars.
—*Fred Allen*

No one goes Hollywood—they were that way before they came here. Hollywood just exposed it.
—*Ronald Reagan*

Hollywood was born schizophrenic. For 75 years it has been both a town and a state of mind—and an industry and an art form.
—*Richard Corliss*, *Time* magazine

[Hollywood] A place where they shoot too many pictures and not enough actors.
—*Walter Winchell*

In Hollywood's heyday, the films were only celluloid, but the cinemas that showed them were marbled citadels of fantasy and opulence.
—*Time* magazine

Show business is dog eat dog. It's worse than dog eat dog. It's dog doesn't return dog's phone calls.
—*Woody Allen* (*Crimes and Misdemeanors*, 1989)

Movie heroes come full circle with Clint Eastwood's filming of *The Bridges of Madison County* in Winterset, Iowa, John Wayne's birthplace. (Painting by Dr. John Tibbetts)

IN THE SUMMER OF 1994, I received a surprise call from Stu Gottesman, vice president and director of field operations at the Warner Bros. studio:

> He said, "Dan, I have some news for you. Clint Eastwood is heading for the cornfields of Iowa, and we want you to coordinate publicity efforts with Marco Barla on the Winterset, Iowa set for *The Bridges of Madison County.*"

This would be a nostalgic event for me because I had grown up in Iowa and was educated there. It was an inspiration to work again with Eastwood's right-hand man, Marco Barla. My office had handled the national premiere of *Bird* (1988) in Kansas City. Also, we had been in many studio meetings together, including one with Clint Eastwood on *Unforgiven* (1992).

Then came the massive amount of publicity that *The Bridges of Madison County* (1995) generated world-wide. The press became a challenge to manage. Reporters from Japan and other countries rushed to Winterset because of interest created by the novel and the production of the film. Traffic jams began to build on the Winterset back roads near the filming.

Each day brought a flood of new interview requests. Newspaper reporters naturally felt as though they were all special cases deserving access to the set and especially to Eastwood. I don't think Marco Barla envisioned such an avid press as in Iowa. The press wanted to interview Eastwood personally on location, and I guess some press felt, as I did, a special bond to a movie being made in Iowa.

THE THEATRE WAS MY TIME MACHINE

Iowa represents a time of innocence to me: a simpler, more optimistic time, a childhood that had predictable rhythms of wakefulness and dreaming.

It was in the darkened theatre that I met my first hero. Little did I know that, many years later, he would become my friend. I imagined what it would be like out there in the galaxies with Flash Gordon or as *Tarzan the Fearless* (1933) or Billy the Kid: all in the persona of Buster Crabbe.

At the same time, I dreamed of riding the dusty plains with a fellow Iowan, John Wayne. Those black and white movie images merged into the sunlight and shadows of my childhood.

My youthful vision of Hollywood centered on events at the local Mayfair Theatre in Shenandoah. The Mayfair Theatre had its own personality with operatic-like balconies and a unique culture of moviegoers.

The theatre was the center of my social world as well as my extended family. When I was banned from the projection room because of the dangers of flammable nitrate film, I would climb back in through a window in the balcony.

The theatre owners were early radio comedians, Tobey and Lindy Stewart, who had two lovely daughters, Kay and Connie. The Stewarts treated me like a son.

Their daughter Kay became a widely known actress in Hollywood. She started in college-theme movies around

1940 at Paramount, and she appeared in such movies as *The Private War of Major Benson* (1955) and numerous TV shows. The most memorable to me was when she was the voice of the Virgin Mary in *The Miracle of Our Lady of Fatima* (1952), produced by Warner Bros.

Early in her career, she became Kay Procter after marrying a son of the Procter family of Procter & Gamble. Paramount News came to Shenandoah and covered the wedding.

THEATRE ATMOSPHERE ADDS TO MOVIE MAGIC

Roy Disney (Walt's brother) told me in my Kansas City office many years later:

> "People love to go to the theatre to be a part of a crowd and also be seen."

It was true in our small town in Iowa. Going to the theatre was an event that seemed to have a certain feeling, the same magic you might feel at a premiere on Hollywood Boulevard. Thursday was family night, and with the smell of popcorn in the air, it was a close-knit community feeling to be in the theatre with friends and families.

Movies at the theatre reminded me of novelist William Saroyan's description of the circus—'adventure, travel, danger, skill, grace, romance, comedy peanuts, popcorn, and chewing gum.' Armond Aserinsky, a clinical psychologist, says further, "From the moment you walk into the [theatre] lobby, the regressive pull of the carnival atmosphere...gives people permission to be in a kind of a childlike state."

The roots of the circus appear in the early days of movie theatre. Kansas City's own American Multi-Cinemas was formed by Ed Durwood—father of Stanley, Richard, and Marjorie (Grant)—and his two brothers. Before 1920, the Durwoods had operated on the traveling tent-show circuit throughout the Midwest and Southwest. Out of those tent shows AMC's worldwide multiplex theater chain was born.

My enjoyment of Douglas Fairbanks, Jr. as *Sinbad the Sailor* (1947) was heightened by the vast and romantic Moorish design of the Mayfair auditorium. Part of the experience was being under an open sky with the clouds and stars projected onto the midnight blue ceiling. The exotic interior world with large stuffed birds perched high in the auditorium was a part of many of my movie experiences.

Afterward, on my late-evening moonlit walks home, I saw my own shadow as if it were outlined by bright sunlight. I saw life as a moving image alternating between shadows and light.

At that time, I had yet to learn the value of publicity in setting up an audience for the enjoyment of a theatre experience.

During my early years in Kansas City, I heard interesting stories about the great Kansas City showman Ed Durwood. I understand Ed used to invite beautiful women as movie guests to be in his theatre lobbies before and between shows to add glamour to the theatre experience.

The Palms Theatre in Culver City, California was another rare cinematic experience.

While living in Los Angeles in the mid-60's, I used to visit the Palms just for the unusual experience. It was run by two MGM actors who made a point of addressing each regular patron by name. One actor sold tickets, greeting patrons at an informal box office, and the other would chat with the audience inside, before the movie started, about upcoming movies and events. Their phone recordings were in Yiddish because of a large Jewish audience. The Palms was a high-touch theatre experience for its patrons.

HOLLYWOOD DEFINED BY DREAMS

The more I learned about a place called Hollywood, the less it seemed like the Hollywood I dreamed about. Ironically, I came full circle to see that, after all, the concept in my youth was accurate.

Hollywood—is it less a place or more a state of mind? Is it an idea, or a fantasy, or both?

> I feel that the heart and soul of Hollywood is where you are as the viewer. It's a place of escape —to fulfill the drama needed in daily life.

No movie experience is complete until it involves an audience. The audience is the only player that varies its role from showing to showing.

It's where movies move viewers, tug at heart strings, and make them part of every action. The Hollywood experience happens when a movie naturally interacts with the audience.

Screenwriter William Goldman said "Movies are a search for past magic." The magic that's produced is the essence of the real Hollywood.

Movies, like art, are personal. Movies are an art form, as a painting is. Yet they are made of pictures that move. The painter or director translates his images into motion for the audience.

Founding studio moguls, such as Adolph Zukor, Samuel Goldwyn, Louis B. Mayer, Carl Laemmle, Cecil B. DeMille, and the three Warner brothers, kept their common touch, born of mostly little-education. They were working-class immigrants, salesmen, and manufacturers who knew what life wasn't and what movies should be. Movies were an idealized life not realized by them or their ancestors in Europe.

DIRECTORS TEST REACTIONS
WHERE THE VIEWERS ARE

The audience interaction is one reason Hollywood executives leave L.A. to test their movies. For instance, director Robert Benton (*Kramer vs. Kramer*, 1979) turned to Kansas City to test audience reactions to his movie, *Places in the Heart* (1984). The purpose is to find what *resonates* with movie goers. This can best be done by leaving the studio environment to experience what fulfills the audience, both its needs and discontents.

After producer Arlene Donovon and others watched the audience response to *Places in the Heart*, they made the cuts based on the research from the preview audience.

Imagine sitting in a 400-seat theatre filled with an audience who doesn't know the film crew is present. It's really an experience to sit by the director and the producer and hear them say such things as, "Cut this scene out. The audience isn't laughing."

When the movie fantasy matches the needs of a particular segment of the movie audience, it becomes a hit.

The studios often found that the perfect place to get reactions to a certain movie was the Midwest. Tri-Star Pictures chose Kansas City as one of five test markets. Gary Marshall, known for his quality pictures, such as *Pretty Woman* (1990) and *Runaway Bride* (1999), came to Kansas City for a test preview of the Tom Hank's movie, *Nothing in Common* (1986).

Later at a studio meeting, Tom Hanks joined our publicists luncheon to talk about the making of *Nothing in Common*.

My experience is that filmmakers sense that the reality of Hollywood is everywhere. On-location filming of movies adds another level of believability to a movie experience.

THE SPIRIT OF HOLLYWOOD IS ALIVE IN YOU

I've worked both sides of the movie business: in theatres and in representing major film studios. First, I was circuit supervisor and advertising director with Dickinson, Inc. Then, I went on to become an executive for Pacific Theatres in Los Angeles.

These experiences equipped me with the first-hand knowledge to represent major studios as a publicist.

For me the most enjoyable part of working on the theatre level is the first-hand experience of getting responses from patrons. Those responses are honest answers as to how well a movie plays, and what makes an audience want to see a particular movie. Such experiences convince me that the true spirit of Hollywood lives in theatres everywhere.

"What is it that motivates people to buy movie tickets?" I asked myself over and over again. Searching for the answer only fueled my desire to make a career in the movie business. Advertising, publicity, and public relations were pieces of the same pie that led me to owning my own advertising and public relations agency dealing exclusively with major studios such as Warner Bros., United Artists, MGM, 20th Century Fox, Paramount, Columbia, Tri-Star, Universal, and Walt Disney.

A MIDWEST METAPHOR APPLIES EVERYWHERE

The use of Midwest Hollywood connections is my metaphor that I believe applies to small towns, suburbia, and cities everywhere.

I've found the magic of Hollywood is borrowed from a variety of sources. These range from where stars come to where movies are made and to where they meet their audiences.

Russell Crowe, from the outskirts of Sydney, Australia, and Best Actor® for *Gladiator* (2000), is an example of a star of humble origins. As he accepted his Academy Award,® Crowe looked back:

> "This moment is directly connected to those childhood imaginings. And for anybody who's on the downside of advantage, and relying purely on courage, it's possible."

9

IOWA—FIELD OF DREAMS

Field of Dreams (1989) captures the spirit of growing up in Iowa. You learn from the movie to have dreams, but to be open to forks in the road that lead to something as good or better.

Hollywood came to Iowa City for the premiere of *Time After Time* (1979). I found it to be a magical evening at the Iowa University president's mansion, followed by an antique car parade to the premiere and an after-premiere Foundation dinner for the University's million-dollar contributors. I was pleased with how smoothly the events flowed with director Nicholas Meyer, producer Herb Jaffe, and other production staff.

The event accomplished two benefits: First, Warner Bros. provided, at no cost, the film for the premiere showing of *Time After Time* (1979). Second, it was a return trip home for Meyer, also a graduate of the Iowa Writers Workshop.

While on the plane back with Meyer, the Kansas City skyline came into view. I happened to mention that he might consider Kansas City as a locale for one of his films. I don't know if that suggestion took, but in 1983 he directed *The Day After*, set in Lawrence and the Kansas City area, for the TV movie about the effects of a devastating nuclear holocaust.

HOW HOLLYWOOD GOT ITS NAME

One day my wife Ruby and I were shopping on Hollywood Boulevard in L.A. when we struck up a conversation with a store owner originally from Kansas City. He told us a fascinating story about how Hollywood got its name. A Kansas realtor named Harvey Wilcox owned a large farm in L.A. His wife overheard a woman on a train refer to the area as "Hollywood." She had apparently gotten the impression of holly trees growing in the wooded area. Mrs. Wilcox suggested the name to her husband and that was the beginning of Hollywood as we know it. It was nice to know that Hollywood owes its name to a Kansan.

William De Mille remembered that Hollywood "was largely peopled by folks from Missouri and Iowa" who moved west to enjoy the California sun and to get away from the Midwest winters.

HOLLYWOOD MAGIC—WHERE IS IT?

The magic of *The Wizard of Oz* (1939) has immortalized deep feelings for Kansas.

Truman Capote brings to life the wintry Kansas prairie with the movie *In Cold Blood* (1967). The actual locales were used, including Holcomb, Kansas, that give a stark reality to the senseless Clutter family murders.

Playwright William Inge's classic *Picnic* (1955) captures a lot of the soul of Kansas. The heart of the movie was the great performances from William Holden and Kim Novak. In 1963, I spent some time at the Columbia studio with co-star Cliff Robertson reminiscing about *Picnic*. Inge was from Independence, Kansas, and five Kansas locations were used in filming *Picnic*.

PAPER MOON SHINES ON KANSAS AND MISSOURI

Called one of the best black-and-white movies of the modern sound era, *Paper Moon* (1973) was filmed near Hays, Kansas and in St. Joseph, Missouri.

Director Peter Bogdanovick (*The Last Picture Show*, 1971) gives glimpses of the 1930's depression across America. *Paper Moon* follows Ryan O'Neal, a Bible-selling con, and Tatum O'Neal as his conniving daughter in her Academy Award® role for Best Supporting Actress.

Much of the filming was done around the St. Charles Hotel in St. Joseph at 5th and Charles Street. The restored dining room seemed to be a natural setting rich in the past. Room 216 was chosen to give the film an elegant effect, partly because of its own fireplace and spacious look.

One of the key sequences was in downtown St. Joseph where bootleggers chased and beat Ryan O'Neal. Vintage automobiles appeared in the background.

KANSAS CITY'S HOLLYWOOD CONNECTIONS

Crime novelist James Ellroy said, "I like to seal myself up—Kansas City is a good place for that—and just think, spend time with my wife, brood, write..."

Although he lives in Kansas City, Ellroy is the L.A.-reared author of *L. A. Confidential* (1997). His noir novel provided the material for the Warner Bros. thriller about crooked cops and Hollywood scandals.

Kansas City scandal has long been a subject for the movies. The K.C. national crime connection was mentioned in *The Godfather* (1972) and had its own *Kansas City*

Confidential (1952), with John Payne, also a noir crime thriller. K.C. native Robert Altman brought crime in the 1930's back to the screen in *Kansas City* (1996).

Producers Merchant and Ivory filmed *Mr. And Mrs. Bridge* (1990), with Paul Newman and Joanne Woodward in the Country Club Plaza area of Kansas City, Missouri. In fact, Newman and Woodward lived in the area during the filming. She was seen by neighbors walking her dog, that is, until the *Star* printed a photo of her dog. Then she could no longer go "incognito."

The film portrayed the late 1930's Kansas City social scene built around the novels *Mr. Bridge* and *Mrs. Bridge*.

In 1976, during the height of the drive-in theatre era, *The Student Body* also was filmed in a mansion near Loose Park. I was part of the group that financed the film. John Shipp was the executive producer. Jack Poessiger, local broadcast movie commentator, appeared in the film.

Another Hollywood connection is Robert Altman who began his success as a director and writer at Calvin Productions in Kansas City. His first big hit, *M.A.S.H.* (1971), starred Elliott Gould and Donald Sutherland. Other Altman hits at the box office include *Nashville* (1975) and *The Player* (1992).

Altman and Elmer Rhoden, Jr. were co-producers of *The Delinquents* (1957). At the time, Rhoden was president of Commonwealth Amusement Company. On meeting him in his Kansas City office, I was impressed with his enthusiasm for his newly formed Imperial Productions, based in Kansas City.

Harlow

The Delinquents, filmed entirely in Kansas City, features Tom Laughlin, who was later widely known as *Billy Jack* (1971).

Alfred Hitchcock became interested in *The Delinquents* and brought Altman to the West Coast. He directed several of the *Alfred Hitchcock Presents* (1955) television shows.

Altman's arrival in Hollywood happened just a couple of years before Kansas City became more important in the minds of the studio executives.

In 1957, Show-A-Rama was founded by two theatre associations to spotlight Kansas City and the Midwest nationally. In order to promote movies to the theatre trade, stars and studio heads came to Show-A-Rama for twenty-eight years. Then the movie industry began to see major changes. ShoWest, the Las Vegas trade show of today, was the result of two primary trends: film distribution being consolidated to Los Angeles and theatre ownership evolving into larger chains.

BIRTHPLACE OF A MOVIE ICON

Mortimer Mouse, one of the biggest stars of all time, was born in Kansas City. The story goes that Walt Disney saw a mouse that inspired him. Walt's brother Roy and Ub Iwerks, their head animator, helped in the creation of Mickey. It happened at 31st and Forrest, just a half block off Troost Avenue at his Laugh-O-Gram studio. Walt also did promotions for the Isis Theatre, located at 3102 Troost.

Often in later years, Walt said about those times in Kansas City:

Portrait of Jean Harlow at the time she was referred to as "Kansas City's Own Star" after the premiere of *Hell's Angels* (1930).

"I hope we never lose sight of one thing…that this was all started by a mouse."

It's no wonder that most of the great cartoon animators came through or got their start in Kansas City. Many got their training through advertising work at the Kansas City Film Ad Company. For example, Ub Iwerks was special photographic adviser on Hitchcock's *The Birds* (1963) and director of Disney's *Skeleton Dance* (1929), and Friz Freleng was creator of Porky Pig. Both came from Kansas City.

MORE MIDWEST CONNECTIONS

The Kansas City area gave to Hollywood such greats as Jean Harlow, Buddy Rogers, Joan Crawford, Larry Parks (*The Jolson Story*, 1946), William Powell, Ginger Rogers, Wallace and Noah Beery, Jim Davis, Craig Stevens, Don Johnson, Dee Wallace, Ed Asner (former president of the Screen Actors Guild), and Dianne Wiest (*The Birdcage*, 1996, and *The Horse Whisperer*, 1998).

Some of the other greats from Missouri are Brad Pitt, Kevin Kline, John Goodman, Chris Cooper, Vincent Price, Craig Stevens, Jim Davis (*Dallas* TV series), and Dick Van Dyke. Virginia Mayo, once described by the Sultan of Morocco as "tangible proof the existence of God," is also from St. Louis. Mayo co-starred in two Warner Bros. pictures with Ronald Reagan, *The Girl from Jones Beach* (1949) and *She's Working Her Way Through College* (1952).

In an interview in 1995 by Kevin Minton, Mayo was asked about Reagan: "Any idea that he would one day be President?"

Inspired by *The Hucksters* (1947), starring Clark Gable and Sydney Greenstreet. The movie is based on a novel by Frederic Wakeman, who is from Kansas City, Kansas, and a graduate of Park College (now Park University), Parkville, Missouri.

Mayo (laughter): "That question is always asked, and sometimes I say, 'Oh yes! I always knew right away that he was to be President. Yeah, I knew.' But I can't say that with a straight face. He was very charming, a sweet man, very honest. I knew he was an honorable person, but I didn't know he'd be President."

Quite a topic of conversation was *Body Heat* (1981) starring Kathleen Turner from Springfield, Missouri. I participated in the studio publicity sessions before its release.

John Huston, director of *The Treasure of Sierra Madre* (1948), was from Nevada, Missouri.

Kansas gave to Hollywood such comedians as Buster Keaton, ZaSu Pitts, and Fatty Arbuckle. Annette Bening, star of *American Beauty* (1999), comes from Topeka. Dennis Hopper is from Dodge City. Kirstie Alley of *Look Who's Talking* Now (1993) and *Drop Dead Gorgeous* (1999) fame is from Wichita, Kansas.

Nebraska has produced great star power for Hollywood. Silent stars Harold Lloyd, Harry Langdon (Council Bluffs, Iowa) along with Marlon Brando, Henry Fonda, Fred Astaire, and Nick Nolte were all from Omaha. Robert Taylor hailed from Filley. 20th Century Fox mogul, Darryl Zanuck, was from Wahoo.

Zanuck handpicked June Haver, from the Quad cities area of Iowa and Illinois, to star in 20th Century Fox Technicolor musicals during the 1940's, such as *The Dolly Sisters* (1945), co-starring Betty Grable. In 1953, Haver, a devout Catholic, joined a convent in Xavier, Kansas for a few months. Later she married Fred MacMurray.

Iowa provided two studio founders. From Ft. Dodge came Samuel Z. Arkoff, co-founder of American International Pictures (*I was a Teenage Werewolf*, 1957, and *The Amityville Horror*, 1979), and W. Ray Johnston from Bristow, founder of Monogram Pictures (Charlie Chan and Bowery Boys 1940's series).

Ronald Reagan, known as "Dutch," spent several years in Iowa as a sports announcer. He worked at WOC radio in Davenport and then at WHO radio in Des Moines. Warner Bros. discovered Reagan and cast him in *Love is in the Air* (1937).

Stars from Iowa included Raymond Hatton (in Hollywood's first silent feature *The Squaw Man*, 1913) who was from Red Oak. James Ellison (co-star of many Hopalong Cassidy westerns) was from Gutherie Center and Dennis O'Keefe (*T-Men*, 1947, and *The Dennis O'Keefe Show*, 1959 TV series) was from Fort Madison. Jean Seberg (*Saint Joan*, 1957, and *Breathless*, 1959) was from Marshalltown. John Wayne was from Winterset. Donna Reed was from Dennison. And Glen Miller was from Clarinda, where annual Miller festivals still occur.

My premise is that talent is still being discovered in the most unexpected places. We never know where it's going to come from. It's just one of the elements that puts the magic into the experience of Hollywood.

Exploring the true Hollywood is an experience in itself. In the next chapter, you will see how publicists make movie experiences come alive.

TWO

How Publicists Add
A Magic of Their Own

What you try to become is a bringer of magic, for magic and the truth are closely allied and movies are sheer magic...when they work, it's, well, it's glorious.
—*John Huston*, Director (*The African Queen*, 1951)

If there's anything I can't stand, it's yes-men. When I say no, I want you to say no, too.
 —*Jack Warner* to a publicist

If nobody wants to see your picture, there's nothing you can do to stop them.
—*Samuel Goldwyn*

Will somebody tell me what kind of a world we live in where some-body dressed up like a bat gets all my press?
—The Joker, *Batman*

I like publicity. I like to watch it operate. When I was bored, I used to drop into the publicity office at Warner Bros. and invent stories. I invented a story about Paul Muni's beard to the effect that Muni had a beard room and that he left the window open and all the beards flew into the ocean. The story got printed.
 —*Humphrey Bogart*

A movie star is a beautiful bubble that's constantly being blown up by a press agent.
 —*Evan Esar*

"Everybody Comes to Rick's,"
inspired by *Casablanca* (1942),
starring Humphrey Bogart and
Ingrid Bergman.

BEFORE A STUDIO GIVES THE GREEN LIGHT to pour millions of dollars into a new movie, answers are needed to these questions:

How will the movie appeal to its anticipated audience by the time it is released?

What will be the appeal of the stars then?

How timely will the theme be?

What other movies will be in competition?

These and other questions face producers daily about the potential drawing power of their movies. Yet as screenwriter William Goldman said:

"No one person in the entire motion picture field *knows* for a certainty what's going to work."

Filmmakers, to resonate with a potential audience, have to be ahead of their audiences. They know what audiences crave, and what will satisfy them.

Hardly anyone in the movie trade would have predicted the success of *American Beauty*. Today, it's hard to believe that Walt Disney's *Fantasia* (1940) failed to find an audience when first premiered.

The making of movies is both an art and a business. These two elements are constantly competing with each other. Even experienced producers, directors, and stars have to deal with both sides, many times not getting their projects financed by a studio. At other times, pictures are approved and made—and still lack audience appeal, or the public tastes have changed.

This is one of the many reasons publicity is so important.

STAR-MAKING MACHINES

Under the management of the studio moguls, such as Louis B. Mayer and Jack Warner, studio experts taught the stars how to dress, how to act, and with whom to be seen in public. Aides and admirers catered to the stars, who became managed properties of the major studios. Producer David Puttnam said, "The studios would test potential talent in a variety of roles, measuring audiences' response through sneak previews, reviews, the opinions of cinema managers, and comments in fan mail."

In the days of the studio system, stars went on regular publicity and personal appearance tours. They had to travel the country to meet the press and their public, unlike today with television and satellite interviews replacing the need to travel. A publicist was always in attendance at these interviews to aid the star and the press.

The studio system was portrayed in Vincente Minnelli's *The Bad and the Beautiful* (1952) and the Coen brothers' *Barton Fink* (1991).

The studios owned a full complement of services: a stable of stars, film production, distribution, and publicity. Warner Bros., Fox, MGM, and Paramount had their own chain of theatres, as well, that ran their own pictures.

Casablanca screenwriter, Julius Epstein said, "Today, each picture is so terribly important for your career. In the old days, your fate didn't hang on one picture. Another one was in production. Another was in theatres."

By 1948, the government forced a divestiture, denying studios control of both film production and theatre ownership. The ruling was known as the Paramount Consent Decree Case, but included, by implication, Warner Bros., RKO, MGM, and 20th Century Fox. Each major studio could no longer count on automatic playdates for their own pictures. Each picture had to be sold based on public acceptance at the box-office.

This decree gave rise to stars becoming the driving force behind their individual careers. Many formed their own production companies, such as Clint Eastwood (Malpaso), Mel Gibson (Icons), and Jodie Foster (Egg Pictures). The decline of stars being produced under the studio system brought stars from other sources, such as Clint Eastwood from the European westerns and John Travolta from television's *Welcome Back, Kotter* (1975).

Today, the stars are more important than ever in the new Hollywood. They have to be "bankable" in order for a producer to get outside-the-studio financing.

Stars in the new Hollywood emerge more rapidly through multi media outlets unavailable in the old Hollywood.

It has always been—and still is—important for a star to have the right publicity for the right movie at the right time to develop or maintain popularity, thus explaining why one star becomes popular while another may not. A personal publicist can be a key adviser to a star's success.

Publicity starts for a movie many times the moment a studio purchases a script or book. The publicity continues each step of the way from production to pre release and post release of a picture.

Personal publicists tout their stars' Academy Award® and Golden Globe caliber performances to voting academy members, the trade press, and key critics around the country. These publicity campaigns become a major influence on the stars' popularity, future marketability, and the amount of money they can demand for upcoming roles.

THE MANY TALENTS OF CLINT EASTWOOD

Frequently the public has a certain expectation from a star, often called type-casting. But the type-casting sets up an expectation from the stars' fans to see them in certain kinds of roles. That's where a theme is important.

Clint Eastwood has made several successful transitions from Dirty Harry movies to *Every Which Way But Loose* (1978) comedies. Then came his later big box office winners, *Unforgiven* (1992) and *Space Cowboys* (2000). Moreover, he is one of the most highly regarded directors in Hollywood today. He is personally involved in the marketing of his own movies.

Nevertheless, Clint has had his box office disappointments. He made films he believed in, such as *Honkytonk Man* (1982) and *White Hunter, Black Heart* (1990). Both were artistic successes; however, Eastwood's fans may have had different expectations than the ones delivered, resulting in less box office success.

JOHN TRAVOLTA—HIS MANY SCREEN LIVES

At the 1977 Show-A-Rama trade convention, I presented my research findings for the national campaign on Travolta's first big successful movie, *Carrie* (1976).

Then he starred in two icon movies of the 70's: *Saturday Night Fever* (1977), and *Grease* (1978). He still was a big star in the 1990's with hits like *Pulp Fiction* (1994), and *Michael* (1996).

However, Travolta has had his less fortunate grossing films, like *Battlefield Earth* (2000) and *Mad City* (1997).

No filmmaker starts out to make a bad movie. Some just end up that way. Occasionally, big stars appear in those limited appeal films who still can't make them into hits. Then the publicists are called in. Sometimes, a solution to gaining appeal lies in the way the film is presented to moviegoers; that's where creative publicity can make a big difference.

Publicity may not always make a film a tremendous hit, but it can cut the size of the losses on a national release.

MOVIES TAKE ON A LIFE OF THEIR OWN

Keep in mind the non-traditional definition of Hollywood: The heart and soul of Hollywood is where you are as the viewer. It's a place to escape, where you fulfill the drama in your daily life.

This definition comes closest to describing generally what publicists do: They capture the drama of a movie and make an emotional connection with the public in their everyday lives.

A CREATIVE CONTEST MAKES A POSITIVE DIFFERENCE

One example of how publicity made a difference was for Tom Selleck's *Lassiter* (Warner Bros., 1984). Along with other cities, we had a kissing contest using a fourteen-foot standee of Selleck's lips. Girls were invited through a radio promotion to participate with this line:

"Be the girl with the most kissable lips."

Scores of avid females got involved in the contest and invited to see *Lassiter* as our guests.

This "kissable lips" promotion resulted in a great deal of exposure through word-of-mouth publicity. There's little doubt this stunt made *Lassiter* bigger nationally than it would have otherwise been.

A PUBLICIST IS AN ALCHEMIST

As an arranger, a publicist links the desires of the press, other media and promotional tie-in partners with items such as books, records, and related products. Publicists seek to build interest and excitement for their product. These promotions benefit each party involved in order to sell a movie or a star to the public.

Publicists are often as much magicians as artists. They weave a magical fantasy around a movie and create a mystique. They get fans to accept the publicists' fantasy as real and maintain their belief in it.

The magic of Hollywood is brought face to face with movie-goers through creative publicity. I use the term "creative" because members of the movie audience are creative in their tastes—continually changing, adapting to trends and creating new directions into the future.

ADDED VALUE OF PUBLICITY

I believe that any movie—or other products or services—can be sold if it is properly presented and then properly promoted to the segment of the audience to whom it is targeted.

Years ago I heard about a 20th Century Fox publicist who talked about his experience as a boy selling pop on the streets of New York. He found that the colder the pop, the more he could charge for it. That type of core appeal or benefit is the "added value" a publicist looks for. We try to "sell the sizzle, not the steak," as salesman Elmer Wheeler would say.

Publicists raise the awareness of a movie or star; they establish a connection with the public. The most vital publicity thrust for a movie is done immediately before and after a movie opens. The star or movie becomes a known quantity, basic to the advertising campaign that follows.

WHAT PUBLICISTS DO

Publicists generate through creativity "an added value" that is not always inherent, either in the movie or in the star. To stay updated, publicists are always on-call for studio briefings on upcoming pictures. Publicists can receive two or more conference calls weekly from a studio.

Here is a list of some of the many activities that a publicist handles:

- Arranging advance critic showings for both print and broadcast outlets before the opening day of the movie. Publicists brief the media with background press kits, television excerpts, and special mailings. They obtain any further information from the studio that is requested by the media.
- Giving feedback of marketing information such as demographic reports, response polls, tracking reports, and obtaining and reporting before and after the movie opens, along with forwarding critics' quotes to the studio.
- Creating "publicity stunts" and tie-in promotions with other partners to extend the reach of the publicity.
- Special interviews of stars or production staff tailored to a particular movie reviewer through interviews in person or by phone.
- Managing personal tours of stars in major cities or scheduling an interview via a satellite television "press tour."
- Inviting the media to press junkets—sometimes to actual locales where a movie was filmed.
- Advance screening programs for research, publicity and word-of-mouth showings sponsored by radio stations.
- Premieres and civic activities.
- Press conferences.
- Providing helpful information to the media.

One key reason publicity remains an important marketing tool is because publicists reach people that paid advertising doesn't. Some people only read the sports section of a newspaper or watch only news programs on television.

A TOUCH OF FAME IN A SMALL TOWN

At the Mayfair, I was surrounded by nationally-known entertainers, such as the Everly Brothers and the Blackwood Brothers. The Blackwoods received nine GRAMMY'S over the years, including "Best Gospel Album of 1966."

Cecil Blackwood was my classmate in Shenandoah until he moved to Memphis.

Cecil's brother, James, told me recently that Elvis Presley's parents had lived in the same housing project as Cecil in 1951-52. Cecil had put together an informal gospel group, "The Song Fellows Quartet," and Elvis had become a part of that group.

Later on, the Blackwoods were asked by Elvis to sing for his mother's funeral. Then, when Elvis died, James Blackwood sang at his service.

We also had a steady stream of cowboy entertainers for guest appearances, such as Lash LaRue, Al Sloey, and Riders of the Purple Sage.

AN EARLY LESSON IN PROMOTION

Robert Waller, author of *The Bridges of Madison County,* mentions my hometown, Shenandoah, Iowa, and local radio station KMA (on page 56 of his novel).

My first experience with creative promotion was as a kid working at the Mayfair Theatre in Shenandoah. The theatre

(left to right) The author, Cecil Blackwood, Ken Turner, Ruby, and James
Blackwood, Jr. during the Blackwood Brother 1983 Kansas City tour.

auditorium served two purposes: it was a live on-stage KMA
radio by day and a movie theatre by night. Live radio broad-
casts from two stations made Shenandoah the Nashville or
Branson of the early radio era.

One of the other stars to appear at the Mayfair Theatre
was Rex Allen, King of the Cowboys, starring in *Arizona
Cowboy* (1950). Republic Pictures had just named Rex
Allen as the new King of the Cowboys after retiring Roy
Rogers. Roy introduced Rex Allen through a short film
used on the screen just prior to Rex's live appearance on the
Mayfair stage.

As my promotion, I had Rex Allen autograph the popcorn boxes to entice each patron to purchase popcorn. It

worked like magic and sales went through the roof. This experience helped create my love for movie publicity. It showed me the power of creative promotion.

SMALL-TOWN MOVIE GIMMICKS

Before television, there were always gimmicks to get viewers back to the theatre week after week, such as the *Screeno*, which was a live-hosted bingo game projected onto the screen. Hollywood Screen Test Night was another promotion. As patrons entered the theatre on Tuesday night, they were photographed. Then the winner's picture was projected onto the screen the next Tuesday.

Other promotions included a Serial Club: pay to see the first 12 chapters of *Batman and Robin* and see the 13th chapter free. Telegram messages from Gene Autry to kids started with "Howdy Partner," that made the kids feel they were getting personal messages from their hero.

A WARNER BROS. LEGEND

So how does this magic happen? It comes from creative individuals like the legendary Marty Weiser of Warner Bros.

Marty joined Warner Bros. in 1936, and subsequently moved to the studio's exploitation department in New York. Then he spent two years in the Kansas City office before he was transferred to L.A. in 1940 as exploitation director for the western states.

A master magician of movie promotion, Marty brought the creative spark from the early studio days of Jack Warner and kept it alive at the studio until just a few years ago.

He worked on special photographic publicity projects with virtually all the major Warner Bros. contract stars, including Humphrey Bogart, Joan Crawford, Lauren Bacall, Bette Davis, and a young Ronald Reagan.

STUDIO CREATIVE SESSIONS

The Warner Bros. national publicity team had no equal in successful movie promotion for many decades. We were fortunate to be at studio meetings from the 1970's to the 1990's under the influence of Steve Ross, who ran Warner Communications.

During the 1980's at Warner Bros., Robert Daly and Terry Semel were the last real studio bosses. They protected the publicists and all other studio personnel from rapid turnovers that occurred at other studios. By contrast, today's studios are small pieces of big companies.

I believe the heart of a major studio's success was the approach used to produce creative ideas. I attended dozens of studio brain-storming meetings of their national and Canadian publicity staffs in Hollywood.

At Warner Bros., Marty Weiser was always there working on his masterful suggestions. Acknowledgments at the beginning of the book lists other publicists in our meetings.

The publicity teams at the studio meetings included a host of first-rate publicists from around the nation. Among the studio staff were vice presidents in charge of advertising and publicity, creative and research directors, producers, directors, writers—and often a star.

YOU'LL BELIEVE MAN CAN FLY

When a box-office blockbuster, such as *Superman, The Movie,* came up for discussion at our studio meetings, the studios fed us a lot of research and creative information on the elements of the campaign so that we could produce relevant publicity ideas.

On *Superman II* (1980), research was used as a blueprint and guide to double check decisions made on the campaign. Research data presenting the creative direction included:

- Advance audience reactions
- Marketing opportunities
- Marketing problems
- Reactions from the theatrical trade
- The movie components (hooks)
- Title test.

Based on this research, rough, unfinished materials were prepared for marketing. Then concepts were refined for final ideas. Audience research studies were done to approximate the real world.

Warner Bros. carried out research with a recruited theatre audience to get actual reaction to *Superman II*. How high or low audience appeal was for this sequel was determined through monitoring studies. Researchers conducted viewer interviews in waiting lines and after the movie.

On *Superman, the Movie* (1979), the Warner Bros. creative director presented the core creative ad line:

You'll Believe Man Can Fly

No actual image of Superman was shown, just the shield. It was better to keep him larger than life in the movie fans' imagination.

Publicity and advertising campaigns were in a constant state of evolving. Tracking studies were done in relation to other competitors' pictures in the movie market place.

After hearing the research and creative platforms, the publicists would bounce new ideas off one another, creating spin-off publicity variations.

The dream factories were the studios, but the meetings served as the idea factories. The atmosphere was open and positive with plenty of humorous one-liners that kept everyone creating. After the meetings ended, the studio staff would edit the ideas and send them back out for national campaigns.

DRAGON GOES UP IN YELLOW SMOKE

After our meeting on *Enter the Dragon* (1973), starring Bruce Lee, Marty Weiser staged a Dragon Race on Hollywood Boulevard.

Marty called the L.A. Chamber of Commerce and offered the use of the dragon from *What's Up Doc?* (1972), for a race against a team of twenty Chinese students and a dragon from San Francisco. Warner Bros. paid for the twenty team members from L.A. and for twenty from San Francisco.

The L.A. dragon led the race briefly, but then stumbled and went up in smoke. The yellow smoke was a great visual for the cameras and the crowd loved it. Marty confessed later that he had planted a yellow smoke bomb in the L.A. dragon. San Francisco won the race but *Enter the Dragon* got the big benefit from the promotion.

Warner Bros. studio publicist Marty Weiser and publicist Don Walker were two predecessors in my area of Missouri, Kansas, Iowa, and Nebraska. Marty Weiser, Don Walker and I formed the continuous line of Warner Bros. publicists in Kansas City that spanned from the early days under Jack Warner to 1998. My predecessors' influence on me has been immeasurable.

A GENTLEMEN PUBLICIST

Don Walker was the 20th Century Fox publicist during the filming of *Jesse James* (1939), in Pineville, Missouri. Later, he joined Warner Bros. in Kansas City and stayed until I took over the publicity activities.

Don worked on many world premiere movies for Warner Bros. He handled the premieres of many of the big westerns with city names such as *San Antonio* (1945) and *Dallas* (1950). He handled the world premiere of *Jim Thorpe, All America* (1951), in Oklahoma. Don was so trusted by Warner Bros. that he was sent personally to manage Natalie Wood on tour nationally for *Rebel Without a Cause* (1955), costarring James Dean.

Don was also responsible for a historic photo shoot of Truman and Reagan together during the Warner Bros. premiere of *The Winning Team* (1952) in Springfield, Missouri. Ronald Reagan was there on the stage, and so was Harry

Truman. It is believed this is the only photo ever taken of Reagan and Truman together.

In *The Winning Team*, Reagan portrayed the story of Grover Cleveland Alexander, the early star baseball pitcher for the St. Louis Cardinals.

In 1949, Don Walker and Marty Weiser combined publicity talents on a national premiere in Kansas City for an independent Lippert Picture, *I Shot Jesse James* (1949).

During the early 60's, Don made an unprecedented station wagon publicity tour for Meredith Wilson's *The Music Man* (1962). He and Leo Wilder, from the Warner Bros. studios visited most towns with newspapers to plant *The Music Man* publicity throughout the state of Iowa, Meredith Wilson's home state.

Warner Bros. has had other great publicists, such as the beloved Frank Casey in Chicago. Casey was a fun-loving publicist in Hollywood as well as in Chicago, and it was Casey who urged the editor of the *Sun-Times* to make Roger Ebert the paper's movie critic. John Wayne, Jimmy Stewart, Lucille Ball, and Jack Webb wouldn't go on tour for a film unless Casey was assigned to the trip. He was that good.

MAGICIANS OF MOVIE PROMOTION

Other names for Hollywood press agents were publicists, exploiteers, and barons of ballyhoo. I call them the magicians of movie promotions. Just like magicians of magic, their secret techniques and working methods have been kept from the public eye.

Publicists came with a certain flair for creating inventive ways to gain attention and interest for a certain movie. Along with their love of the work, their mission was—and still is—to sell tickets.

Studio publicists serve three distinct publics:

- Communicate the benefits of a picture to the movie trade.
- Communicate a picture's values to the press and other media.
- Capture the imagination of the movie fans and sell the movie—making them want a movie-going experience.

The individual spirit is the greatest force behind a publicist's creativity. The best publicists never worked only for money. They communicated their love for the movies through their work with the public.

In the next chapter, the publicist's techniques are revealed that sell stars and movies to the media (magazines, newspapers, television, and radio). However, the ultimate purpose is to gain popularity for the stars and their movies with movie fans at-large.

With Steven Seagal, on tour to promote his first
movie, *Above the Law*, (1988) from Warner Bros.

With Tim Conway, on tour to promote
The Prize Fighter (1978), co-starring Don Knotts.

THREE

Ways Publicists Create Star Power

I think people need something to look up to, and Hollywood was the
only royalty America ever had.
—*Bette Davis*

Thank you. You [Julia Roberts] are Horse & Hound's favorite actress.
You and Black Beauty. Tied.
—*Hugh Grant* at a press junket, *Notting Hill* (1999)

One day cock of the walk, next day a feather duster.
—Tina Turner eyes Mel Gibson,
Mad Max Beyond Thunderdome (1985)

Doing a full day of interviews at this level, the feature film level ...
well, it's a matter of how much silliness you can put up with. I mean,
these guys ask a stupid question...and then sit back, very proud of themselves.
—*Russell Crowe* about a TV reporter as told to Robert Butler, *Kansas
City Star, L.A. Confidential,* interview.

I am big. It's the pictures that got small.
—*Gloria Swanson* to William Holden, *Sunset Boulevard* (1950)

A man kept saying to me: "you're a star, you're a star." I thought: this
year I'm a star, but what will I be next year—a black hole?
—*Woody Allen*

The smaller the star, the bigger the car.
—Anonymous

An actor is a guy who, if you ain't talking about him, [he] ain't
listening.
—*Marlon Brando*

A celebrity is a person who works hard all his life to become well
known, then wears dark glasses to avoid being recognized.
—*Fred Allen*

MOVIES ARE STARS. The moguls who founded the movie industry knew that the real draw for movies, in their pure essence, were the Stars.

Film critic, Alexander Walker, saw stars as reflections of the needs, drives, and dreams of the movie public. Critic Raymond Durgant suggests that stars are mirrors for their movie fans, and in those mirrors they adjust their self image through their reflections. Stars condense real characteristics of movie fans, or compensate for any absence.

It's no wonder that the best publicity tool for a new movie is the star, co-star, or the creative staff behind the production.

Star names stimulate the interest of the movie-going public and the coverage by the press. Russell Crowe, during an *L. A. Confidential* press interview for *The Kansas City Star*, offers his view:

Russell Crowe, during *L. A. Confidential* (1997) media interviews in Kansas City.

"The pure definition of what I do is take lead roles in feature films—so I guess by definition my job is to be a movie star."

Stars, such as Crowe, offer a "trademark" quality when used to add value to a production. Names with a track record always enhance "insurance value" at the box office.

Some of the stars we've arranged for the press to conduct face-to-face interviews are Clint Eastwood, Chevy Chase, Kevin Costner, Julia Roberts, Danny Glover, Mel Gibson, Sylvester Stallone, Arnold Schwarzenegger, Gene Hackman, Robert Redford, and Barbara Streisand.

A Kansas City contribution to these New York and L.A. press interviews was movie artist, Dr. John Tibbetts. The paintings in this book display the talent he brought with him, revealed

Halle Berry, on Kansas City press tour for *Strictly Business* (1991).

through a surprise portrait of the star being interviewed and later autographed.

The publicist is the advisor for the star while on tour. Halle Berry is a celebrity who projected "star power," and the press could feel it as she entered the Ritz-Carlton for a conference on *Strictly Business* (1991), in Kansas City. Halle made a significant comment about success when she said:

> "People need each other to reach certain goals. When they are extremely successful, they rarely do it alone. They have help from other people."

If stars have financial interests in a film (such as having put up personal money or having contracted for a percentage of the gross), they may also be directly involved in the publicity and promotion.

Occasionally, a star becomes directly involved as Charlton Heston did on the movie, *Mother Lode* (1982). Heston took a hands-on approach; he contacted the media and arranged his own interviews. Such a bold approach by a famous personality can work publicity wonders for a movie. This kind of bonanza will help make a great track record for a new movie, especially for a picture that's harder to market.

With Michael Moore, on tour for *Roger & Me* (1989).

Another was Michael Moore, basically a one-man mission with his film, *Roger and Me* (1989). First, he put together a production team and sold them the idea. Then, he used all types of creative methods to sell the idea to the people of Flint, Michigan, so they would help finance his movie venture through bingo games.

Next, he sold the completed film to Warner Bros. This way he was assured that a national Warner Bros. publicity team would be behind it. Warner Bros. sent him on a personal tour around the country publicizing the film. After Michael's tour a group called Roger's Rangers did follow-up publicity on

Roger and Me. They were a team of production experts and associated staff from Flint, Michigan.

Those kinds of self-starters that you find in Heston and Moore are rare. When they do show up, the results are most often phenomenal.

How do the critics and other journalists make actual contact with the stars? How do they interact, and get quotes that can be used in the press, including radio and television? Since the media is the bridge between the movies and the public, such contacts can prove to be of immeasurable help to the publicist in reaching the actual movie-going public, the ticket buyers, the popcorn eaters, the adoring fans.

There are four primary tools that publicists use to inform the media.

1. PHONE INTERVIEWS

All over the country, radio hosts or print journalists conduct interviews by phone for live or taped radio programs. For example, we arranged a phone interview, called a "phoner," for Robert Butler, critic of *The Kansas City Star* to talk with James Ellroy, author of the crime novel, *L.A.Confidential*. Ellroy called Butler for the interview from the Toronto Film Festival prior to the opening of the movie, *L.A. Confidential*.

The radio phone interview can accommodate quick changes in a star's schedule; it allows for greater flexibility. Moreover, radio interviews in smaller cities, especially on country and western stations, are fabulous for country-related movies.

Phoners are used for interviews with directors while they are in production on a new movie. It is a method of getting advance reaction on how their ideas in a film might be accepted.

2. SATELLITE PRESS TOURS

The name of this category is really a misnomer. Nobody actually travels or "tours!" The star sits in a chair in front of one camera, for instance, in Los Angeles or New York, and gives a personal five-minute interview to perhaps thirty or forty cities over the course of the day. Through an elaborate pre-arranged schedule, the star's image is down-linked by satellite to the various TV stations that are participating. The stations up-link the critic's voice in order to enable a two-way conversation. Nobody actually travels. The star does not actually tour. It's all done electronically.

One down-side is that the interviewers may feel a lack of the personal touch they would get from a live interview. No doubt many of these satellite managers still put personality and fun in the interview to help make up for the lack of face-to-face interviews.

This method of star "tours" is growing and will become even more popular in the future. Satellite press "tours" offer many advantages: less cost with no travel expenses for the studios, and the stars' convenience of avoiding the rigor of a national personal tour. Local critics like the idea of this method because they do not have to take time away to fly to another city. Satellite interviews solve many problems.

3. PERSONAL APPEARANCE TOURS

This one is *not* a misnomer. These stars really do travel. They fly from city to city, giving live interviews for several weeks promoting their films.

We hosted dozens of such personal visits by such stars as Russell Crowe, Cicely Tyson, Robert Conrad, Harry Dean Stanton, Robby Benson, Nanette Fabray, Buster Crabbe, George Peppard, Dick Clark, "Wolfman" Jack, William Marshall, Jodie Foster, and Dale Robertson. Incidentally, those stars often told fascinating stories during these tours, and I'll be revealing some of these in subsequent chapters.

Rush Limbaugh, before his national success in New York as America's top radio host, interviewed movie celebrities on tour while he was a Kansas City radio host. He interviewed Buster Crabbe at KUDL-AM about his physical exercise book *Energistics* (1977), and he had Nanette Fabray on his KAYQ radio show about her new comedy *Harper Valley PTA* (1978).

Our agency usually arranged a breakfast or luncheon press conference for the personality tours. This technique allowed for six to twelve press members in a single conference. Usually, as a publicity tool, a video was made of the entire session.

Personal promotional appearances by stars, with critics and other press, have always worked well for film publicity and always will, but perhaps the biggest and most legendary promotional event is the press junket.

4. PRESS JUNKETS

A junket is a "promotional event prior to the release of a motion picture during which the stars and filmmakers sit in hotel rooms for several days while ... journalists from all media interview them."

Notting Hill confides with movie fans about what happens at press junkets with the burden of interviewer's questions, embarrassing tabloid headlines and other celebrity occupational hazards. It's almost a self portrait of Julia Roberts. She plays an international star that makes fifteen million dollars a movie. At her press conference, she is shown in her sunglasses going room to room to do press interviews.

The press junket was again the subject of satire in *America's Sweethearts* (2001), starring Julia Roberts, Catherine Zeta-Jones, and John Cusack.

We have made arrangements for the press to go on hundreds of such junkets. They sometimes are held in conjunction with film galas such as the Toronto Film Festival.

Junkets are carefully choreographed events. Studios invite press to L.A., New York, or to unusual filming locations, even to other countries to interview stars, directors, writers, and production staff. Junkets are usually held on weekends. One day is used for television critics and another day for print press.

Terry Press of Dreamworks Pictures said about junkets:

> "It's often the only chunk of time the stars will give, and a lot of magazine shoots and other busi-

ness takes place within the parameter of a junket that wouldn't be as easy without it."

Dana Kennedy reported in the *New York Times*:

"Entertainment reporters are ushered into a 'hospitality suite' with buffet tables full of food, drinks, and fantastic desserts and given goodie bags of promotional paraphernalia like baseball hats and T-shirts.

Often, studios join together and "piggy-back" their junkets, so critics may do interviews for two or three films at the same hotel in one weekend.

Warner Bros. held their *Man Without a Face* (1993) junket with Mel Gibson in Bar Harbor, Maine, where they had shot the film. The press members enjoyed a lobster dinner near the ocean with Mel Gibson, a highlight of the junket.

Junkets can be quite eventful. One critic attended a *Without a Clue* (1988) junket in London. Michael Caine and Ben Kingsley were available for interviews at the Grosvenor House in the Mayfair district, but this critic was also able to interview Sir Arthur Conan Doyle's only living link: Dame Jean Conan Doyle. He visited the Sherlockian sites in London. The press was treated to a farewell banquet, and the critics all had their own personal waiters.

For another twist in junkets, Warner Bros. conducted interviews on the actual noir, drippy, watery sets used for

Lethal Weapon IV (1998). The interviews with Mel Gibson, Rene Russo, Chris Rock , Joe Pesci, Danny Glover, and martial arts wonder Jet Li, were taped on the actual Warner Bros. sound stage where the picture was filmed.

Julie Warner, on Kansas City press interviews for *Doc Hollywood* (1991), starring Michael J. Fox.

Sometimes critics go to exotic places to do interviews. For *Memphis Belle* (1990), the critics were sent to Memphis where they got to see the original plane. Puerta Vallarta, Mexico was the setting for the junket for Kevin Costner's *Revenge* (1990).

As noted earlier, we sent press from all over the world to Winterset, Iowa to interview Clint Eastwood while he was making *The Bridges of Madison County*. The setting, with the bridges and colored leaves, made an interesting and beautiful October background for the interviews. Television critics aired their interviews back home, and many a reporter printed fine articles in their local papers and magazines.

Studio publicists have held press junkets for decades, and there's no question that these are a superb benefit to the promotion of the films. The critics fly to their destinations, stay in the best of hotels, eat the finest cuisine, enjoy the best vintage wine, and get to meet our nation's royalty: real live movie stars.

Face-to-face conversations are the most personal of Hollywood's public relations techniques used to reach the movie business trade, the media and the general public. Warner Bros. used this method to introduce such new faces such as Steven Seagal, Robby Benson, Halle Berry, and Julie Warner.

The studios roll out their top talent for studio meetings and conventions put together for the movie trade. Hollywood's biggest names grace the stage to promote their latest films in Las Vegas annually for the ShoWest trade convention.

BEHIND THE SCENES: UP CLOSE AND PERSONAL

The following seventeen selections are a collection of celebrities we've worked with on press tours, at events, and in studio meetings. One of the joys of a publicist is working with people. Two were real studio moguls and two were personal friends. The selections cover messages they passed on, the stories they told, and the memories they left.

ERNEST BORGNINE

Whatever it is women like, I ain't got it.
—*Ernie Borgnine* as *Marty* (1955)

IT WAS A PLEASURE to have Ernest Borgnine, one of the Hollywood greats, on a personal appearance tour. He was a regular guy with exceptional communication skills and fun to be with during radio, TV, and newspaper interviews. Although in Kansas City for an exploitation film called *Devil's Rain* (1975), he made the best of it and everyone loved him.

A highlight was our lunch at the Hereford House restaurant and Borgnine telling about an incident in Mexico City after the release of the Best Picture *From Here to Eternity* (1954). In that film, he played Sergeant "Fatso" Jackson, a real tough alley-type fighter.

Ernie had gone into the Marie Esabelle Hotel restaurant. He noticed that all the waiters and cooks had huddled back in the kitchen. When they were coaxed out of the kitchen, they came into the dining area with meat cleavers and knives ready. Why? Because as "Fatso" Jackson, in the film, anticipating having Frank Sinatra in his care, he had snarled:

> "Tough Monkey. Guys like you end up in the stockade sooner or later. Some day you'll walk in. I'll be waiting. I'll show you a couple of things."

With Ernest Borgnine, on press   53
tour for *Devil's Rain* (1975).

Obviously, the waiters and cooks had seen the movie and were frightened. They thought Borgnine was really as mean in real-life as "Fatso" was in the movie. It's a good example of how a movie can influence reality.

We talked about a tough-guy role Borgnine played in another movie, *A Bad Day at Black Rock* (1955), starring Spencer Tracy. He developed quite a reputation as being one of the best bad guys in Hollywood.

As our conversation continued, we talked about *Marty* (1955), his Oscar winning role as Best Actor® of the Year. He won against some pretty long odds too. James Dean and Frank Sinatra were nominated as best actor the same year.

As Borgnine and I both recalled, Harold Hecht, James Hill and Burt Lancaster had produced *Marty* as a small picture without any thought of it becoming a hit. It proves the old movie business axiom: "You never know where a hit movie is going to come from."

I set up Borgnine's personal appearance tour with Rick Kallet at Bryanston Pictures. Rick later became head of co-op advertising at Warner Bros., and we had a good working relationship for almost 20 years.

Incidentally, the 1975 picture, *Devil's Rain,* was a story of a group of Satanists on-the-loose in a rural countryside. The most memorable aspect of this movie was that it was John Travolta's first feature-film role in a bit part.

american
CLASSIC SCREEN

VOLUME ONE, NUMBER 6   JULY/AUGUST 197

FLASH GORDON RETURNS!

. . . interview with Buster Crabbe

ANNOUNCING:
. . . publication of a major
film history classic.
See page 32.

Tibbetts

BUSTER CRABBE

It was a great strip [Flash Gordon], but for a picture?
I thought who would sit still for it? Crazy.
Too Fantastic. I even thought I might just
give it all up and go back to stunt work.
—*Buster Crabbe*

BUSTER CRABBE AND I were long-time friends, first meeting at Universal Studios in North Hollywood.

On one occasion, Buster and I met at Universal City during the taping of a tribute to Muhammad Ali at the Universal Sheraton Hotel. I discovered that Ali and I shared the same childhood screen hero, Buster Crabbe.

King of the Jungle (1932) was Buster Crabbe's first Paramount feature, in which he played a "lion man."

Buster was a great Olympic Champion swimmer, and he explained:

> "I swam my way into the picture business. My whole life was changed by one-tenth of a second."

Buster played Tarzan in the movies and is perhaps best known as Flash Gordon in the great serials. Maybe some of you saw him on television as Captain Gallant in the Foreign Legion. Buster Crabbe was one of the great men of action films. He looked great in tights and had lots of adventures in rocket ships with lovely Dale Arden.

For *Raiders of the Lost Ark* (1981), Steven Spielberg and George Lucas were inspired by Buster's role in the serial *Flash Gordon Conquers the Universe* (1940).

American Classic Screen magazine cover of Buster Crabbe, known as "King of Movie Serials," as Flash Gordon, and an image of him as he appeared in 1977. Flash Gordon © King Features Syndicate.

Best Man Picks Best Woman—Actor Buster Crabbe with Capt.
Jeff Latz chooses a queen for the Wentworth Military Academy Ball.

When I asked Buster to be best man at our wedding in 1977—he gladly said, "Yes." Since he was set to do a book tour at the time, I offered to arrange a publicity schedule for him in Kansas City.

His new book was *Energistics* (1977), a work that outlined his theories on physical fitness. What Buster did not know was that in addition to our asking him to be best man, our agency would also be asking him to select a beauty queen.

Each year we asked Warner Bros. to furnish a Hollywood star to look through several photos and resumés to pick the queen for the Wentworth Military Ball in Lexington, Missouri. In past years, we had such star-judges as Robert Redford and James Caan; so this year we asked Buster to be the judge since he was already in town. He selected a lovely young lady, and *Boxoffice* magazine, a Kansas City-based national trade publication, covered the story. Buster was featured with a photo and article. The caption was "Best Man Picks Best Woman," a nice reference to his role in our wedding.

The year was 1977, the time of *Star Wars*. My movie-artist friend, John Tibbetts, painted Buster as he appeared in 1977 along with his Flash Gordon image for the cover of *American Classic Screen* magazine. Because Tibbetts was also writing a Buster Crabbe article for the magazine, he conducted an interview in Buster's room at the Alameda Plaza (now Fairmont) in Kansas City. What resulted inside the July/August issue was a five-page article with seven photos of Buster. Significantly, Buster made nine serials, the most for any leading man. The article was especially important because it went into detail about his B westerns, the least covered of Buster's films.

In 1996, the July/August issue of *Films in Review* magazine published its "From the Olympics to the Silver Screen" issue. This issue contained another John Tibbetts profile of Buster Crabbe in connection with events surrounding the upcoming marriage to my lovely fiancée Ruby Scott, who would later join the agency to become a valuable partner in our Hollywood publicity efforts.

Picture of our wedding party during the ceremony at Unity Village. Some of the celebrities include:
1. Buster Crabbe, 2. Rush Limbaugh, 3. Poet James Dillet Freeman.

Tibbetts

WALT DISNEY (AND HIS BROTHER ROY)

It has that thing—the imagination and feeling of happy
excitement—I knew as a kid.
—*Walt Disney*, at Disneyland opening

WHEN I WAS A CHILD, my first experience with
movies came when my father, a contractor, was partially paid
for a job with a can of films and a hand-crank movie pro-
jector. The can contained silent Mickey Mouse cartoons,
tinted in a peach color.

The images of that time are burnt into my memory.

> When I was about five, my father and I would lie
> flat on the living room floor. We projected those
> Disney cartoons onto the ceiling over and over,
> for hours at a time.

> Those animated images, as they flickered onto the
> ceiling, fascinated me, and are still as vivid today.
> The light and shadows from that toy projector and
> those Disney cartoons helped to shape my life.

In 1963, I was in L. A. for the *Motion Picture Herald*
[trade magazine] Conferences that held meetings at each
major studio. The purpose was to exchange ideas and build
a better relationship between theater owners and the movie
studios. It brought us in contact with the top actors and stu-

Portrait inspired by an innocent-
looking Walt Disney, about the
time he left Kansas City for
Hollywood.

dio executives. I represented Dickinson Theatres as circuit supervisor and advertising director.

There was another purpose—to sell the stars and their upcoming movies.

Before going to the Disney studio, we had been in meetings at Universal. We had spent time earlier in the day with Gregory Peck who was at a closed private studio showing of *To Kill a Mockingbird.*

Then we had meetings with Tony Curtis (*Captain Newman, MD*, 1963) and Universal executives. Tony Curtis impressed everyone with his depth of knowledge of the theatrical market. He amazed us with his facts and figures on boxoffice results of current movies.

Gregory Peck's co-star, Angie Dickinson, was at Universal promoting *Captain Newman, MD*. Barbara Eden (*Seven Faces of Dr. Lao*, 1964) was there with husband Michael Ansara.

We also enjoyed conversations at the Disney studio with many of the greats, such as Ed and Keenan Wynn (both in *Son of Flubber*, 1963), and Robert Taylor (*Miracle of the White Stallions*, 1963). In those days there was a greater need for studios and stars to market their product on a one-to-one basis.

On the same occasion, I walked into a room with only one person present, who turned out to be Sabu (The Elephant Boy) from the original *Jungle Book* (1942). We talked about our concepts of God and Sabu's life in India.

Then he said to me:

Author, at right, with celebrity couple Barbara Eden and Michael Ansara at Universal studio session of the *Motion Picture Herald* Merchandising conference.

"If you were a little boy riding on an elephant in India and someone tapped you on the shoulder and asked you if you want to be in the movies, would you believe in God?"

It was magical visiting with Sabu, but something more magical was about to happen.

Walt Disney walked right up to Sabu and me and started talking about upcoming projects at the studio. He continued to talk with us for probably half an hour.

My impression was that he seemed less like Uncle Walt on TV, having more energy and greater personal intensity. Disney told us he had just finished looking over the projects being done at the studio. I had a sense that he was probably deeply involved in the projects, managing even the smallest of details. It was doubly satisfying to meet him. He was a giant in the industry; yet he had publicized movies on the streets of Kansas City where he had his roots.

We talked for some time about his early days in Kansas City. I mentioned the Cauger Family for whom Disney had worked. He actually worked for Vern Cauger at the Kansas City Film Ad Company, where Disney worked on cartoon commercials for local businesses. He asked how the Caugers were.

Then a couple of his animators from Kansas City joined our conversation.

One of the reasons we were there was so that Disney could report to theatre owners on the progress of *Mary Poppins* (1964). Ub Iwerks, Walt's old friend from Kansas City and early chief animator, was there working on combining live action with animation sequences of *Mary Poppins*. We were able to watch part of the live action on the closed set; as it turned out, *Mary Poppins* made a fortune for Disney.

Also, Disney introduced us to his new process called "animatronics," that animate actual life-like figures. We saw close up his moving and talking figure of President Lincoln. This Lincoln figure captured the public's imagination at the 1964 New York World's Fair.

We visited the office of Ub Iwerks where he was developing the scenes for Alfred Hitchcock's *The Birds* (1963). The innovation of these processes was one of the key steps that Disney made toward producing creations closer to actual life.

Seeing Disney's Lincoln figure and animatronics tied in with another purpose for my trip to Los Angeles for Glen Dickinson, Sr., of the Dickinson theater chain. I was to survey the potential of a wax museum for Kansas City; so I had meetings with the owner of the Hollywood Wax Museum.

I had read a magazine article about artist Madame Stuberg and her fine designing of life-like wax figures. I finally located her in an old Hollywood warehouse through the help of a latter-day silent movie theatre owner, John Hampton.

I was delighted to meet Madame Stuberg and see her works-in-progress. She told me about Jack Warner hiring her to design the wax figures, although uncredited, for 3-D thriller *The House of Wax* (*1953*), starring Vincent Price. She also mentioned that actor John Barrymore used to come over to the studio "to sleep off the night before" among the mannequins and props.

As I recall my studio visit with Disney, he showed us story boards for Disney projects that were planned for the next ten years or more. Later an interview was given by Dr. John Tibbetts in Kansas City that described Walt's use of story boards in all of his planning, for his movies, Disneyland, and his other parks, as well as his own life.

A story board is a glorified cartoon strip, and many of Walt's were as big as a wall, describing hundreds of movie shots and incidents. Many hours' worth of film can be read at a glance.

Tibbetts continued by saying:

> "The story board becomes a metaphor: how to plan costs, how to achieve efficiency, how to give proper direction to a life as with movies.

> "We can look at Disney's life too as a story board. We skip from one movie to the next, from one decade of his life to the next. We see the total picture of creation of life itself. A remarkable thing about Disney is that he created not just motion pictures but also places to live, and lifestyles for others."

Some seeds of Disney's visions were planted early. As a boy, before moving to Kansas City, he lived in Marceline, Missouri. It was probably there that the Disney dream took root for Main Street USA in the Magic Kingdom.

About three years after meeting Walt Disney, I was in the advertising agency business in Kansas City, located next door to the Disney office. There, on two different occasions, I had long conversations with Walt's brother, Roy. He came to Kansas City to keep up friendships in banking circles downtown and to visit family.

As I mentioned earlier, Roy Disney told me that in the movie business you can always count on human nature and people wanting to get out to a theatre to be seen and to be a part of a crowd. In talking about the lasting appeal of theatres, he said:

> "People have a stove at home, but they still enjoy going out to eat. If a lady gets a new outfit, she'll want to show it off in public."

With Mark Harmon, promoting *Beyond the Poseidon Adventure* (1979) at the
Show-A-Rama Theatre Owners Convention in Kansas City.

MARK HARMON
(AND PRODUCER: IRWIN ALLEN)

You have celebrities, and you have actors. I want to be an
actor. I want to find out the extremes of what I can do.
The uncertainty is the reason I love it.
—*Mark Harmon*

THE FIRST THING I can say about Mark Harmon is that
he was his own person. He knew not to take his press releases too seriously.

In fact, concerning his studio photo, he said with a grin
while shaking his head, "Publicity!"

His amusement about the obligations of publicity came
from exaggerated fictional reports about his being in love
with Angela Cartright, just because the two played romantic leads in *Beyond the Poseidon Adventure* (1979).

Fame was always a part of his life because his father was
Tom Harmon, the famous football All-American from
Michigan. His mother was the widely known actress, Elyse
Knox, who played in twenty-two movies, including *Joe
Palooka in Fighting Mad* (1948). His father, Tom Harmon,
played along with Elyse Knox in *Sweetheart of Sigma Chi*
(1946).

Mark Harmon was a successful football player at UCLA,
but he found time to develop his interest in acting through
college productions.

Warner Bros. sent him to Kansas City in our care for the 1979 Show-A-Rama movie convention. He received the "Male Star of Tomorrow" award at the convention.

Ruby managed his activities at the convention, and laid out his media schedule to promote Irwin Allen's upcoming Warner Bros. release *Beyond the Poseidon Adventure.*

Because Harmon had not seen the finished movie, he expressed concern about how it turned out and how it would be received by the public.

Later, we handled an advance research showing of *Beyond the Poseidon Adventure* at the Glenwood Theatre in Overland Park, Kansas. Irwin Allen came quietly into town for the showing.

A couple of humorous moments came during Irwin's visit.

First, we had booked dinner for him, his two studio publicists Tony Habeeb and Bob Frederick, and Frank Wells, president of Warner Bros. During the evening, Irwin became quite annoyed at the trio playing at the restaurant, and he posed a question to one of his assistants:

> How much do you suppose the musicians would take not to play?

Later in the theatre, we all watched reactions of the audience to the film, *Beyond the Poseidon Adventure*. The picture was just ending, and someone at the back of the theatre stood up and yelled:

> "You should pay us to see this piece of crap!"
> Amid other negative comments, Irwin Allen &

Company quietly slipped out the back door without people really knowing anyone from the studio was there.

After the screening, everyone left the Glenwood Theatre in a rain storm. Just as Irwin's limo pulled onto the highway, a speeding car rear-ended it. Studio publicist, Bob Frederick and I were in a car just behind the limo, and Irwin's publicist, Tony Habeeb, was behind us. We all jumped out to see if anyone was hurt. Irwin said "no" and refused any emergency assistance. My feeling was he didn't want anyone to know he was in Kansas City for the advance showing.

Irwin and his wife rode back to the Crown Center Hotel with Bob Frederick and me.

Years later, Ruby and I visited Irwin in his office at the Warner Bros. studio, where he was a charming and gracious host. He showed us his production planning room which he called "The War Room" and his elaborate filing system of color-coded boxes. During our visit, we chuckled over the events of that night in Kansas City.

With an animated Ice-T, in a Kansas City press conference for *New Jack City* (1991).

ICE-T

I mean I like Spike [Lee] but I'm more for action, I would
rather see Steven Seagal do some karate.
—*Ice-T*

ICE-T CAME TO SPREAD THE WORD in Kansas City
about his movie *New Jack City* co-starring Wesley Snipes.
I found him straight-forward and dedicated to a positive purpose. He stated, "*New Jack City* is a story of a gang group's
discovery of crack and their attempt to move into the
megatude of big-time drug dealers." Ice-T told about a bold
publicity showing for the picture:

> "We screened *New Jack City* for like 400 gang-
> ster-loving beeper-carrying, gun-packing hustlers
> in New York and Los Angeles. At the end of the
> movie, when Wesley Snipes (as Nino) dies, they
> cheered. They were cheering themselves getting
> killed."

Ice-T describes further his intent to evoke reaction at the
New York and Los Angeles advance showings: "This movie
works—it's point-blank in your face, that if you mess around
with crack, you're gonna die."

He told us that the movie makes kids think, even though
it doesn't hit some of them until later, and that the message
of the picture may not get to them until it's bounced over
from one of the other kids who did get the point.

73

Ice-T is known as the father of "gangsta rap." He was one of the original rappers. He said this movie is for the same audience as his music fans.

He explained further:

> "My whole career is built around kids from my neighborhood, the kids that nobody else really cares to aim at.

You get insight into what drives these kids—the mentality and the money. You see that Wesley Snipes, as the arch criminal in the movie, is just a capitalist."

Then Ice told what he thought *New Jack City* would do for Black-White relations:

> "I think it can only help, because the only way you're gonna help relations between the races is if people understand each other.
>
> "That's all it takes; right now people just don't understand each other.
>
> "You don't know what it is to be Black. I know how Ozzie and Harriet lived. I know all about being White because I watched it on TV. But you guys don't see us in our own environment trying to fight our own problems. The Vietnam vet that's a drug dealer doesn't like it either. Not all Black people are drug dealers. Some Black people hate drugs more than White people could possibly imagine.

"Maybe Whites don't understand that we're trapped, too. Maybe we can all help each other. So, hopefully, you won't look at the TV next time and say, "You know why they're selling drugs, cause there's tens of millions of dollars in it. They're socially down. Their back's up against the wall, and right now crack and cocaine is the number one employer of minority youth.""

At the end of the press conference, Ice-T said:

"I wish there was a movie you could take kids to and they would stop drugs for life and stop stealing and stop going to jail."

With animator Chuck Jones, at the national press conference kick-off of the re-
release of the classic Warner Bros. cartoons at AMC's theatres nationally.
(Photo by Dave Venner, *Entertainment Spectrum,* Vince Koehler, producer.)

CHUCK JONES (ANIMATOR / DIRECTOR)

Of course, you know this means war!
—*Groucho Marx* (borrowed by Bugs Bunny)

IN 1990, I INTRODUCED cartoon animator Chuck Jones to the Kansas City press and the theatre owners on behalf of Warner Bros. in celebration of Bugs Bunny's 50th Birthday. Also at the same time, there was a press conference in Kansas City to announce that AMC theatres were going to exhibit nationally the reissue of the original Warner Bros. classic cartoons.

This event spread from Kansas City to the national press across the country.

Jones continued animating the old Warner cartoon favorites, Bugs Bunny, Daffy Duck and Porky Pig. He added his own characters that became popular favorites, Wile E. Coyote, Henery Hawk, Marvin Martian and others.

Jones said, "I have a lot of ties to the Kansas City area." His mother was born in Nevada, Missouri and grew up in Chanute, Kansas. One of his uncles was a reporter with *The Kansas City Star.*

Undoubtedly, Jones was one of the most celebrated original directors of Bugs Bunny at Warner Bros. He applied certain rules and disciplines to the Warner Bros. characters.

What sets these Warner Bros. cartoons apart? He said, "The key to the whole matter is the personality of the characters, not the drawing." He brought out the subtle shadings within the personalities of his cartoon characters. Then he pinpointed his working philosophy:

> "I'm principally concerned not with what Bugs Bunny is, but with who he is. I want to get inside him and feel him from my viewpoint."

Discussing the art of cartoons brought him back to the Midwest art connections:

> "A lot of people don't realize it isn't only cartoons that originated here, but also great artists in residence happened all through the Midwest and along the Mississippi.
>
> We probably wouldn't have had artists such as Thomas Hart Benton and Reginald Curry, and people who were supported by the government. Even the great Mexican artists were brought up here by the Works Progress Administration. So at this time, as to whether we should support artists, I believe it's vital."

Jones told of Kansas City's long cartoon history. As Butch Rigby of the Thank You, Walt Disney group says, "Kansas City may not have been the birthplace of animation, but it has been the 'cradle of animation.'"

Many of the animation greats started in Kansas City with Walt Disney. Ub Iwerks, his chief artist, and Friz Freleng along with Rudy Ising and Hugh Harmon all followed Disney to Hollywood.

Freleng, after leaving Disney, became one of Warner Bros. most prized directors. He became known for his classical and popular musical cartoon sequences, precise staging and sharp comic timing. Freleng created some of Warner Bros. most beloved characters: Sylvester, Tweetie Pie, Yosemite Sam, and Porky Pig. After Warners, he created the Pink Panther for Blake Edwards.

When he came to Kansas City in 1990, Freleng said, "Kansas City is quite a breeding ground for real talent." He continued, "Porky Pig was created right here in Kansas City," in his old neighborhood near the Country Club Plaza area around 45th and Mercier.

> Freleng said, "Two kids I used to play with were fat kids. One was called Porky and other was called Piggy. I had a vision for a cartoon strip. I never thought of movies, because they were extreme. Yet it got to the screen before it got to the newspaper."

STANLEY KUBRICK

[Stanley] has an adroit intellect, and is a creative
thinker—not a repeater, not a fact-gatherer. He digests
what he learns and brings a new project an original point
of view and a reserved passion.
—*Marlon Brando*

IT WAS IN THE FALL OF 1977, I received a call from
Leo Wilder, Warner Bros. director of field operations:

"Expect a call from Stanley
Kubrick in London. Kansas City is
one of three cities he's picked to
search for a boy to play in one
of his upcoming pictures. The
other two cities are Denver and
Chicago."

In a few days, I did indeed receive a
call from Kubrick. We found out that
this search was for the future release of
The Shining based on Stephen King's
book.

© Warner Bros. Museum
of Modern Art Archives

Kubrick greeted me in a friendly manner saying,
"I want to run an ad in *The Kansas City Star* next
week for a young boy between the age of five and
seven with a Midwest accent to star in my upcoming picture."

Then we worked out some copy by phone and finally he said that he would fax further suggestions to me.

I asked that our company name be carried in the ad. And he jokingly said:

"Oh, you want some free advertising?"

"Of course", I replied, and he did let us include our name.

Then he added:

"I am sending my assistant, Leon Vitali, to conduct the interviews of about 500 boys."

He said he would check back with me on the final copy and cordially said goodbye.

What came next was the methodical way in which Kubrick worked. I received a series of calls from at least four assistants of Kubrick's inner circle. Each one had a script of questions posed by him, and they all wrote down my responses to each question and reported directly to Kubrick. I sensed they were under pressure to get things right for him.

The ad ran, and I received another call directly from Kubrick about running it a second time to fill the interview schedule; so we repeated the first ad.

Kubrick's personal assistant, Leon Vitali and his wife Kersti arrived with the interview schedule. In advance of Leon Vitali's arrival, we collected parents' applications and photographs of their young sons.

Before meeting Vitale, I hadn't realized he was an actor as well. We had handled Kubrick's *Barry Lyndon*, released by Warner Bros. in 1975. Leon played Ryan O'Neal's maltreated stepson, Lord Bullingdon. The beautifully done film portrayed Ryan O'Neal's conflicts with Leon Vitali.

Vitali video taped an interview with every boy on our list doing improvisational acting. Leon said Stanley wanted an accent somewhere between Jack Nicholson's and Shelly Duvall's. These interviews were sent to Kubrick in London for review. Kubrick chose five-and-half-year-old Danny Lloyd from a railroad family in Chicago. Vitali stayed on as Danny Lloyd's acting coach during production.

In 1999, I was surprised to see Vitali was again personal assistant to Kubrick on his final movie *Eyes Wide Shut*. Also in the film, Leon played Red Coat, the leader conducting the trial at the secret cult proceedings against Tom Cruise at the mansion.

Among our first house guests in our present Kansas City home were Leon Vitali and his wife, Kersti.

Vitali spent about three weeks in Kansas City conducting the interviews before he and Kersti returned to Sweden.

Even though they held hundreds of interviews here in Kansas City for the young boy in *The Shining*, Danny Lloyd of Chicago ultimately was the one who got the role.

IN KUBRICK'S VIETNAM, WIND DOESN'T BLOW. IT SUCKS

In 1987, another Kubrick picture that we handled was *Full Metal Jacket*. Leon Vitali was again casting director on the picture. Kubrick had announced to the world press that he was seeking eighteen-year-old men who could play a Marine. After a wave of tapes, Stanley had Vitali invite professional actors to apply for the roles.

Arliss Howard from Kansas City played the Cowboy character, but the centerpiece character of the movie was the real-life former drill instructor Lee Ermey who came on a personal appearance tour with us.

If you've seen *Full Metal Jacket*, you know how riveting Lee Ermey was in his portrayal. We enjoyed his prankish, versatile sense of humor when we worked with him. Ermey was really playing himself in the first half of the movie, using the name of Gunnery Sergeant Hartman, a punishing hard-driving D. I. (Drill Instructor), but the real-life Lee Ermey was a lot of fun.

Ermey was chosen to lead the publicity charge for Kubrick in the United States and abroad. However, at first he was to work only behind the camera, then he described how his playing Hartman on screen actually came about:

> "The casting director had all these young guys who were being considered as extras, and they had me play the D.I. and yell in their faces while it was being videotaped.
>
> I yelled for an entire afternoon, and the next day Stanley told me he was so taken with my colorful language that he had a transcription made from the videotape. It came to 45 type-written pages of insults."

Thus Ermey's dialogue was put into the script; he was technical director and was cast as Hartman.

Having fun in Kansas City with Lee Ermey, who headed the *Full Metal Jacket* (1987) publicity push in the United States and abroad for Stanley Kubrick.

Ermey gave me a lot of insight into how detailed and methodical Kubrick operated when putting a picture together. Here's how Ermey worked with Kubrick:

> "I went over the script with Kubrick with a tape recorder. I would do the scene the way I wanted to do it and then get Kubrick's suggestions. I talked through the best dialogue lines and worked

with them. Then, I worked up an outline for the scene. I placed an asterisk by the questionable parts.

"One reason we got along so well was that whenever I wanted to get rid of a scene, I came up with two or three alternatives so that Stanley would have different ideas to choose from.

"Then I used a black book of names of guys I knew in Viet Nam to get authentic scenes and words. I got a consensus from several individuals and worked out an outline. Kubrick is a word-for-word person. As a D.I., I built credibility and then shocked them."

Kubrick was fiercely concerned with the accuracy of the small details that made up the background of his films because he felt this helped the audience to believe in what they saw on the screen. He wanted men who could walk the walk and talk the talk.

Lee Ermey said that Kubrick was a genius and lived by the motto: "No pain, no strain, no gain."

In our Kansas City office in 1978, about the time Rush interviewed Nanette Fabray on KAYQ Radio for *Harper Valley PTA*.

RUSH LIMBAUGH
(a.k.a. JEFF CHRISTIE)

[Rush:]   Is it true things have gone to the dogs
                in Hollywood?
[Nanette Fabray] I didn't know they had.
—Harper Valley PTA (1979) radio interview

ONE SUMMER DAY in 1975, I was listening to disco on radio KUDL-FM, in Kansas City. Between records, I heard what seemed to be the most outrageous phone-in conversation ever:

A lady was telling the disc jockey:

> "My parents went on vacation and left me to baby-sit the dogs! And I'm going to sue them!"

The announcer broke out in laughter. Then the lady barked back to the disc jockey:

> "Watch your peas and cucumbers!"

That was my first introduction to Rush Limbaugh, also known as Jeff Christie to his loyal Kansas City radio audience.

Because of my movie background, I could see that Rush is an entertainer with a flair for showmanship. From the beginning, he had a natural talent for promotion.

In 1993 Rush was in Kansas City reminiscing about old times with Dr. John Tibbetts for a television program, *Heroes of All-Time.*

John Tibbetts:	"You've known Dan and Ruby how long?"
Rush:	"Well, how did this happen? Back in '75 I got to town, in '76 at radio KUDL... there was an account executive who kept coming back after having met with Dan, 'This guy [Dan] loves you, Rush, this guy loves you.' We eventually had lunch and a good friendship was born out of commonality of political views and sense of humor. Dan may not remember this, but he probably was the first guy to recognize the talent I now have a chance to employ. He wanted to put me on television as the reincarnation of Joe Pyne. He had a tough time getting some headway for that, but I think he's the first guy who really thought there's more to this guy than just this radio show. He was the first guy to spot it."
John:	"Only the first of many kinds of interesting conjunctions of people and events. For example, you and I and Buster got together."
Rush: (Laughs)	"Keep the Joe Pyne thing in mind. When I first got here, I was an insult guy like Pyne, and Dan saw a connection, I didn't want to be abrasive, but management of the radio station knew that would cause a reaction."

John:	"Abrasive?"
Rush:	"Oh, abrasive, insulting, combative, argumentative I would hang up on people. I'll be honest. During the days KUDL was disco, that's what it was, so Dan said this guy would make a great Joe Pyne, so that's the image I had.'
	So here comes Buster Crabbe, a good friend of Dan's, a wedding, so he's gonna be best man and I've got this talk show. KUDL—still an AM station out there in the cornfield off of 435 South."
John:	"Really?"
Rush:	"Really, I'm in there. I'm waiting. I've got things all set up and you and Buster and Dan are driving up the gravel dusty road and Buster stormed in just prepared for bear.
	Dan's prepared him that I'm this insult guy, that I don't care who Buster Crabbe is. It's no big deal to me. I'm not impressed. And it was the strangest hour."
John:	"Flash Gordon [Buster Crabbe] turned out to be a pretty nice guy?"
Rush:	"Oh he was. It was all in fun. It was a memorable experience for me. You were there, trying to plug your own book, while I was supposed to be interviewing Buster, so you were in fine form."
John:	"One of these experiences you thought best not to have?"

Rush: "You must understand something, I was 25 or 26, Dan Meyers was one of the leading advertising agency people in town. His reputation was superb. To have him befriend me, he was really the first business man in town to have befriended me and it meant a lot to me. Then, he invited me to be in the wedding and said that Buster is gonna be best man.

Again my perspective, getting in town, not mattering a whole lot to anybody, still trying to carve my own niche, and here I am being given the opportunity to be included certainly in one of this city's biggest events in terms of society, and to be a part of it was a big thrill and to meet Buster Crabbe and to have him treat me as a justifiable member of the wedding party—it was something I will never forget."

Rush Limbaugh, as he appeared as a groomsman in our wedding.

Rush Limbaugh was a fascinating personality even back then, and who would have dreamed of the success he was to achieve with his syndicated talk show? I'm proud to have known him "when."

GEORGE MILLER, DIRECTOR
(Mad Max 2: The Road Warrior)

There's a dark side to all of us collectively, which we confront in our mythologies. People say, "You must be very
interested in violence." And in a way I am, but in relationship to death. I worked as a doctor for two years…
—George Miller

WHEN AUSTRALIAN GEORGE MILLER got off the
plane in Kansas City, it was to be the day he learned of the
accident on the set of his latest film. It was July 25, 1982.

A helicopter had crashed, killing actor Vic
Morrow and two young children. It had hap-
pened during the nighttime filming of
Twilight Zone—The Movie (1983).

Although George Miller directed the air-
line sequence of *Twilight Zone—The Movie*,
he was here to promote and oversee the U.S.
release of his film, *The Road Warrior*
(Originally *Mad Max 2*, 1981). He appeared
on the NBC TV noon news and kept focused
on his purpose describing the clips from *The
Road Warrior* as they were shown; yet it was
clear that he was eager to get back to the
hotel to talk with his partner, George Kennedy, to see what
reports he had on the accident.

© Warner Bros., Museum of
Modern Art Archives

George Miller represents to me an outstanding example

of compassion and persistence. In Australia, he became a medical doctor and spent a lot of time in emergency rooms treating all sorts of athletes with broken bodies in battered uniforms. That evening in our home over tea, he told us these experiences gave him the idea for the persona in the original *Mad Max* (1979).

His persistence as a physician carried over into his motion picture work. He went from the challenge of hospitals to the challenge of putting together, financing, and making his first movie, *Mad Max*.

The Road Warrior, like the original *Mad Max*, takes place in a vast wasteland left after years of world warfare and economic collapse. The director described why he thought *Mad Max* was a success:

> "There are a couple of reasons, one technical and the other mythological. On the technical side, there's the fact that I tried to make the picture without much dialogue. Talking just isn't important to an action film, and I've always been a big fan of silent movies.
>
> "I've watched a lot of silent movies and tried to understand the syntax of film—the film language—which is cross-cultural. I tried to envision my two films as silent movies. If the story made sense visually, then any sounds we added could only help it."

According to what he told me, I believe *Mad Max* moved

Mel Gibson from being a stand-up comedian in Australia to becoming an international action star.

Miller met challenges that kept him and investors from doing it the easy way, which might have led to failure. He pursued the political influence of an important investor who would put in $400,000, but the investor had an alternate motive. He wanted to keep control, and he kept maneuvering in that direction, until finally Miller and the group met the challenge. The investor would distribute the picture, but Miller's group had to get the other investors before he would put in his $400,000.

It was also interesting that Miller mentioned that George Lucas and Steven Spielberg used *Hero of a Thousand Faces*, a book by Joseph Campbell as basis for the heroes and villains in their movies. It was the message of ever-recurring mythological heroes and villains in life.

In the director's own words about the international success of the *Mad Max* image:

> "The mythological thing is something that became apparent only after we realized that Mad Max was going to be a hit. For instance, the Japanese related to it as a samurai movie. The Europeans saw it as a futuristic spaghetti western. Max is a kind of wandering knight, and that image appeals to virtually every culture. I've seen African tribesmen who understand every moment of Mad Max, and they didn't speak a word of English."

Mad Max II: The Road Warrior (1981) hot car promotion
sponsored by KYYS radio at the Bannister Mall Shopping
Center parking lot in Kansas City.

Michael Moore of *Roger and Me* (1989), as John Tibbetts interviews
him for *The Christian Science Monitor* in our home.

Michael Moore, between interviews, with Tom Blanck,
Warner Bros. Field Representative.

MICHAEL MOORE (ROGER & ME, 1989)

> Well, the million tourists never came to Flint.
> The Hyatt went bankrupt and was put up for sale,
> Waterstreet Pavillion saw most of its stores go
> out of business, and only six months after expecting a
> million people a year to go to New Jersey to
> Chemicalworld, or a million people going to Valdez,
> Alaska for Exxonworld. Some people just don't like to
> celebrate human tragedy while on vacation.
> —*Michael Moore, Roger & Me*

MOORE WAS AN INDEPENDENT guy who made an independent film—very independent. He called it *Roger & Me* because it was a pseudo-documentary about Moore trying endlessly to get a personal interview with Roger Smith, Chairman of General Motors.

Michael's rationale? G.M. had closed its huge plant in Flint, Michigan (Michael's home town) throwing thousands of auto employees out of work. Moore then became a self-appointed crusader on behalf of those newly unemployed and made humorous attempts to force the G.M. top man to make some explanation. The result was Moore's serio-comic movie, *Roger & Me*.

The day Michael Moore got off the plane in Kansas City wearing his "Gone Fishin'" hat, I knew we were in for a good time.

On the way into town, I told him of the many great things

97

about Kansas City: more fountains than Rome, more boule-
vards than Paris, and the world-famous Country Club Plaza
shopping area. I was told recently he still jokes in his dry
manner about this spiel I gave him.

Before he checked into his hotel, we headed to the
University of Missouri—Kansas City to visit a film class.
The eager class members had just finished watching *Roger
& Me* on 16mm film.

Moore held a question-and-answer session. The talk was
stimulating but humorous, and he had excellent rapport
with the class. About fifty eager students heard his viewpoint on what happened to the citizens of Flint.

Even after Moore left town, follow-up publicity occurred
with "Roger's Rangers," made up of Flint citizens who publicized the picture through radio, television, and appearances
on behalf of the opening of the film.

The opening of *Roger & Me* was filled with irony, to say
the least. A large auto plant in Kansas City had recently
closed, leaving hundreds of disgruntled locals out of work.
Moreover, it was a G.M. plant, and the parallels with the
Flint situation were painfully obvious. Thus Moore's film
arrived in a very timely manner.

The one big parallel with Kansas City and Flint was in
the question: "Why were these plants closing?" This question was behind Michael Moore's crusade to get answers
from G.M. chairman, Roger Smith.

Roger & Me exploited the reality that Smith was unavailable to Moore for three years. In fact a seat was reserved
for Roger Smith at every theatre on opening night. But all

that was seen was the solemn cardboard figure in a roped-off seat.

I felt at several points how much Moore's story reminded me of a friend of mine mentioned earlier, radio's Rush Limbaugh. Rush had a lot of bad luck on jobs years ago in Kansas City when he was unknown, but both Rush and Moore developed a new way to present public issues through humor.

Rush once told me about his philosophy on the use of humor. He thought of it as being backed by an element of truth. He seems to use his creative instincts when behind the microphone to employ humor in an intentional way, often by talking about serious subjects, yet making his points through the use of humor.

Moore made his film on a shoestring. He actually raised the $160,000 through garage sales and bingo games, and he filmed in 16mm.

He stresses the importance of "… keeping your sense of humor when coping with depressing times …" and he compared this view with Charlie Chaplin's philosophy. Moore said Chaplin dealt with the poverty of the depression in a humorous way in *Modern Times* (1936), and with Nazi terror as he played Hitler in *The Great Dictator* (1940). Moore pointed out that Chaplin knew he had to use humor to deal with serious themes; so Moore followed suit.

One final incident illustrates the casual irony and humor of Michael Moore. When I brought a local newspaper critic to the hotel for a scheduled interview, I sent someone up to Moore's room to check on him. He opened the door, just about ready to put on his shoes, except for a small problem. He had only one sock. After a little help and lots of looking, the other sock surfaced just in time for the interview. It was an ordinary day in the unusual life of Michael Moore.

He liked to tackle the most serious of subjects with an approach that comes naturally to him: humor. And that's how he left Kansas City, looking back with his head cocked, a gleam in his eye and a touch of devilish humor!

PEGGY REA

Having a full figure has one advantage [she laughs]. It
makes me look younger than I really am because the
wrinkles just don't show on a full face.
—*Peggy Rea*

SHE'S HELD EVERY JOB in Hollywood except being
a grip, but she said:

"Believe it or not, in all my time in the business,
this is my first press junket. Press junket—sounds
like a dessert, doesn't it?"

She is best known to audiences
for her two popular TV roles
—sweet, placid Rose in *The
Waltons* and the outrageous Lulu
Hogg in *The Dukes of Hazzard*. My
favorite Rea film was *Cold Turkey*
(1971), filmed in Winterset, Iowa,
about a whole town that quit smok-
ing. She played the wife of the
nervous surgeon.

Peggy Rea, during a press tour in
Kansas City for *In Country* (1989).

Peggy Rea came to Kansas City
to publicize her film *In Country* (1989) starring Bruce Willis.
She played Mamaw, a Kentucky farm wife who lost her son
in Vietnam. During the movie she was driven to the Vietnam
Veterans Memorial in Washington, D. C.

She described the experience at the memorial:

"It's a most unusual place. I don't care when you go there—day or night, hot or cold—there will be somebody there who lost somebody whose name is on the wall, friends, relatives. They leave incredible things there: not just flowers, but also military medals, photos, letters from kids to fathers they've never seen. All with no thought to ever having them returned. There's a room nearby where the Park Service keeps all that stuff that's been dropped off."

Peggy Rea also performed on stage in Kansas City during the early years in *A Streetcar Named Desire* along with Anthony Quinn.

THE GOLDEN AGE OF MGM MUSICALS

What I found most interesting was her beginning a career as a secretary at MGM, where she worked with famed musical producer Arthur Freed. She worked there during the time of production of *Meet Me in St. Louis* (1944) and *The Harvey Girls* (1946).

Rea told of a great, memorable moment for her—being one of the first to hear the hit song *On the Atchison, Topeka and the Santa Fe* played by Johnny Mercer on the office piano.

Rea described the MGM office parties at actors' homes as one-of-a-kind events with their biggest stars performing just for their private gatherings. Fred Astaire, Gene Kelly, and Judy Garland shared their talents at such gatherings. It was just like one big beautiful and joyful family!

Speaking of Arthur Freed and MGM, Nanette Fabray came to Kansas City to promote *Harper Valley PTA* (1978). Fabray starred in *The Band Wagon* (1953), the last great MGM musical which was directed by Arthur Freed. She sang *Louisiana Hayride*, and along with Fred Astaire and Jack Buchanan, she sang *Triplets* and the film's biggest number, *That's Entertainment*.

Just as in her movies, Fabray was delightful, and rose to each occasion with grace and quiet charm.

Working publicity with Peggy Rea and Nanette Fabray gave us a chance to relive magical moments with stars that were a part of the great MGM musical era.

With Ruby and Nanette Fabray, at the American Restaurant in Kansas City during the press tour for *Harper Valley PTA* (1978).

Christopher Reeve as Superman, on the cover of *American Classic Screen*
magazine in 1979. © Superman the Movie. TMS & DC Comics Inc.

CHRISTOPHER REEVE

I asked the director, Richard Donner,
if I were going to have to wear a "silly suit" as the young
Superman. I really didn't want to wear one.
Seriously, the only person who looks decent in it
is Christopher Reeve. He looks great.
—Kansas City's *Jeff East*
(Superman as a boy)

CHRISTOPHER REEVE WAS SUPERMAN. However, he flew to Kansas City on the Warner Bros. jet, this 6'4" rising star of *Superman: the Movie* (1979).

Reeve stayed at the Westin Crown Center where he conducted a full itinerary of press interviews. Upon arrival in the hotel lobby, a woman came up and asked him to describe her undergarments; an obvious reference to Superman's x-ray vision in the movie. He seemed less than amused.

Again he was approached by a couple of convention fans in the lobby asking if he would pose for a picture with them. At that moment, they discovered their camera batteries were low and Reeve patiently waited for the husband to go to a nearby gift shop for replacements. They were impressed by his consideration and sincerity.

Reeve's trip to Kansas City was two-fold: He came on a promotional tour for *Superman—the Movie* and to receive a medallion of honor from the Show-A-Rama convention

With Christopher Reeve, at Show-A-Rama autograph-signing session.

of movie exhibitors (theatre owners). That evening he participated in the final tribute called "An Evening with the Stars." He shared the stage with Alan Alda and Dyan Cannon.

About his role as the man of steel, Christopher said:

"I wanted to return to a late '40s, post-war image of a hero, but I wanted to stay away from a macho character. Superman is a pacifist who would never take advantage of another person."

He continued:

"I feel that the Superman role is one part in a series of parts I'll play over a lifetime. My life is really a work in progress. There may be a price I'll have to pay for being in the limelight, but it's very small in comparison to the rewards."

HOW COULD THIS HAPPEN TO SUPERMAN?

Christopher Reeve is the finest example of a screen hero becoming a real-life hero. When he was on tour with us at age 26, he was bigger than life, handsome and healthy. Suddenly on July 27, 1995 near Charlottesville, Virginia, he was almost killed when he was thrown from a horse. Although paralyzed from the shoulders down, he continued to develop his talent with bold efforts at acting and directing. Also Reeve turned his injury into a new opportunity to find a cure for paralysis caused by a spinal cord injury through the Christopher Reeve Paralysis Foundation.

While in Kansas City, he said,

> "I learned that acting was like a credit card, enabling you to go anywhere in your imagination and explore other cultures. To me, the idea of let's pretend is as basic as a heartbeat."

At the end of the Show-A-Rama banquet of 2,000 people, we cued him that it was time to leave for the Kansas City municipal airport where the jet awaited. What an experience it was to roll onto the darkened runway in a long black stretch right up to the Warner Bros. jet as it was ready to whisk Christopher Reeve back to the world of Hollywood.

STEVEN SEAGAL

I get compared to Clint Eastwood. It's flattering, but I don't
like it for a lot of reasons. One is it makes me uncomfortable
in the sense Clint is a legend in his own time.
And I'm, you know, some piss ant.
—*Steven Seagal*, *Above the Law* (1988) press conference

TALL AND MYSTERIOUS and a little stand-
offish, Seagal's charisma captivated the interviewers. Steven Seagal was not widely known
when he arrived in Kansas City to promote his first
movie, *Above the Law*.

The Warner Bros. sales department told us that
the studio had spent $100,000.00 on Seagal's
screen test, the most that a studio had spent since
the golden years of Hollywood. We had found when Warner Bros.
sent a personality on tour, the prospects were generally quite
good.

After watching his interaction, I could tell he was going to
have great appeal for the action-movie crowd.

He confided his approach to acting during a breakfast press
conference:

> "Not that I think I'm a great actor, but I have not spent
> a lot of time on techniques. I think the cerebral
> approach to technical acting is very difficult to watch.

"A lot of people have acted—spent a lifetime growing up in schools—very technical approach —trying to imitate the role and not understand it.

"James Mason taught me more about acting than anyone else. James said:

"'You have to really, completely, absolutely understand the role—to become one with it.'"

Above the Law was not just "make believe" for Seagal. He is a 6th-degree black belt in Aikido and is a master at a wide variety of martial arts. He said it is also called "the Christian martial art" because an attacker is defeated by his own momentum and violence.

Seagal's Aikido background reminded me of several years prior, when we had a personal tour of Master Bong Soo Han for *The Trial of Billy Jack* (1974). Han was Tom Laughlin's trainer for the film. He was also the first to bring Aikido from Korea to America. Off-screen, Seagal says he puts more emphasis on his spiritual and intellectual development than the physical.

Seagal is an expert marksman and master of weaponry. He used all his hands-on life experiences in Southeast Asia to make the movie. We could sense he was the real thing.

He admitted that the action in *Above the Law* isn't real martial arts, but just street fighting. He said if you want real martial arts, check out a video copy of Akira Kurosawa's *Red Beard* (1965).

Our first press interview for Seagal was with Robert Butler, critic of Missouri's *The Kansas City Star* newspaper.

Seagal's magnetism continued throughout the day at a large noon press conference and other face-to-face interviews.

He was interviewed by Andrea Stewart of the Kansas City, Kansas newspaper, *The Kansan*. He told Andrea that he would name a character after her in one of his upcoming pictures, and he did. The character was played by Kelly LeBrock in Seagal's second Warner Bros. film, *Hard to Kill* (1990). Incidentley, at that time, Kelly LeBrock was Seagal's real-life wife.

The last time I saw Seagal was at the ShoWest Convention held during March 1997 in Las Vegas. He came surrounded by security in his Indian buckskin jacket he wore in *On Deadly Ground* (1994).

Before he came on the stage, Robin Williams and Billy Crystal were poking fun at Seagal, imitating him by beating on a tom-tom and making cracks about his acting. When Seagal came to the microphone, he looked down at Williams and Crystal and told them:

> "You guys better shut up or I'm going to mess you up!"

He was indeed an imposing figure!

With Steven Seagal, at a breakfast interview for *Above the Law* (1988), with Robert Butler of *The Kansas City Star*. Bob's daughter Blair is beside Seagal.

At a one-hour lunch press conference for Steven Seagal, with round-robin questions from several Kansas City area newspaper and cable interviewers.

JOHN TRAVOLTA

I feel best when I'm creating—because that's me.
That's my identity. When a lot of people try to confront
their lives, they try to separate themselves
from their work. They say, "I am going to work things out
without that dependency." Well that's [bull]. Because
what you do is what makes you alive.
That's what makes you great.
                              —*John Travolta*

JOHN TRAVOLTA HEADLINED the 1985 Show-A-Rama convention (theatre owners) and trade show held in

Author, left, with John Travolta and Ruby Scott Meyers, at the Show-A-Rama convention in Kansas City.

Kansas City. He had an extremely easy manner as well as a real style that was genuine and down-to-earth. I handled part of the national campaign on *Devil's Rain* in connection with Ernie Borgnine. It was John Travolta's first feature movie.

Seeing him at Show-A-Rama brought back memories of an advertising presentation I made to the convention on one of Travolta's earliest movies, *Carrie* (1976). The findings on the appeal of *Carrie* came from our research with film classes at the University of Kansas.

In the Show-A-Rama presentation, I introduced a "Strategy Selling Concept" for marketing movies to college students in different regions of the country. The first step involved a questionnaire completed by university students. The second step was a review of the results by a team of psychologists, professors, students and theatre exhibitors. This approach helped *Carrie* find a bigger targeted audience in the Midwest.

Many years earlier, I handled the national premiere of *Prime Cut* (1972), a Lee Marvin and Gene Hackman film from National General Pictures, partially filmed in Kansas City, around 5th and Main in the market area. I held a press conference at the Hereford House steak restaurant for the premiere, pairing "steak" with *Prime Cut.*

Sidney Ganis, from National General Pictures, came into town to work the press conference. Ganis was to become president of Paramount Pictures and later associated with George Lucas.

We were so hard-pressed for stars from the movie that National General Pictures sent in two young women who played bit parts. One was a girl from Overland Park, Kansas, and the other was a sweet, skinny Texas girl who played "Poppy" in her first movie, *Prime Cut*. It was Sissy Spacek.

Our agency participated in the national success of *Carrie* that brought both Travolta and Spacek together in one movie.

We also handled a personal press tour for John Heyman, the producer of the docu-drama *Jesus* (1979) from Warner Bros. Here again was another Travolta connection. Heyman was the New York consultant who put the finances together for *Saturday Night Fever* (1977) and *Grease* (1978) which became Travolta classics.

DEE WALLACE (STONE)

I was dismayed when secretive Spielberg
[E.T. Director] refused to show me the script.
When he relented and let me read it behind locked doors,
I was hooked. The character [a mom] was struggling,
emotional, strong, with a sense of humor.
And she was pretty, not beautiful.
—*Dee Wallace Stone*

TO PROMOTE STEPHEN KING'S *CUJO* (1983), Dee
Wallace Stone came to us on a Warner Bros. publicity tour.
It was a homecoming for her as well, since she was from
Kansas City, Kansas—adjacent to Kansas City, Missouri,
just on the Kansas side of the state line.

Her husband, Christopher Stone, who appeared in the
film, accompanied her on the trip to Kansas City. They had
both starred earlier in *The Howling* (1983) and were asked
to do *Cujo* at the same time.

In *Cujo*, Wallace plays a woman trapped in a car trying
to protect her little boy against a rabid dog. She said it was
the hardest thing she had ever done.

"I've got to say, I usually hate what I do," Dee said, with
a serious look. "I'm my worst critic," she said, smiling.
"When I saw it [*Cujo*] at a screening, I was peaceful. I think
it's good. As for my performance, I think I've run my best
mile."

Beside Dee Wallace, Judge Cordell
Meeks, Jr., National President of the
American Lung Association (2001-
2002) and his wife Mary Ann at the
Indian Springs Theatre autograph-
signing session for *Cujo* (1983) in
Kansas City, Kansas.

I remember it was a hot Summer day. She had a full day of interviews with *The Kansas City Star*, *The Kansan* (The Kansas City, Kansas newspaper), and radio and TV stations, including an American Cablevision interview on the front steps of our home.

Ruby and I owe a lot of thanks to Dee Wallace and Christopher Stone. They were the motivating inspiration for us to complete all seven phases of a self-improvement course in "Conceptology." In particular, I remember an instructive conversation I had with Christopher at our dining room table that convinced us to continue the course to its completion.

Dee talked about how the courses helped her form an "image" of what she wanted in a film role. Her "image" came true with the role of the mother of three children in Spielberg's *E.T.: The Extra Terresterial*.

Further about her philosophy, she said:

> We have within ourselves a universal knowledge,
> a sensitivity about everything. All we have to do
> is to have the confidence to allow ourselves to
> take advantage of it.

We ended Dee's publicity tour with an autograph-signing session and a showing of *Cujo* at the near-by Indian Springs theatre. At the signing session, Dee was presented the key to the city of Kansas City, Kansas by District Court Judge Cordell Meeks, Jr. Mayor Ron Mears presented Dee with a framed proclamation declaring it "Dee Wallace Day."

JACK L. WARNER (The Last Mogul)

You were very good playing a bitch-heroine, but you
shouldn't win an award for playing yourself.
—*Jack Warner* to Bette Davis

I never stabbed Jack Warner...only in my mind
—*Bette Davis*

© Warner Bros. Museum of
Modern Art Archives

ONE OF MY MORE MEMORABLE
VISITS as a theatre-chain executive
was to the Warner Bros. studio. It was
one of a series of face-to-face meetings
arranged to promote an exchange of
ideas between theatre executives and
management of the major studios.

An ironic thing happened just two
nights before at the Beverly Wilshire
Hotel. We attended a banquet for *The
Great Escape* (1963), with Steve
McQueen on stage. During the cere-
monies, John Ford singled me out of the
audience, came over and greeted me with a handshake. You
may remember him as the director of one of America's
favorite movies *The Quiet Man* (1952), starring John Wayne.

The next day at Warners, I met Maureen O'Hara. Seeing
her in person was even better than on screen in *The Quiet
Man*. I was captivated by her delicate Irish complexion set

off by her radiant auburn hair. No wonder she was known as one of Hollywood's most beautiful actresses.

Even though others were invited to meet the Warner Bros. stars, only two of us showed up as they appeared at an empty sound stage. Alsong with Miss O'Hara telling about her upcoming *Spencer's Mountain* (1963) with Henry Fonda, we talked about drawing-board pictures with Jeffrey Hunter (*King of Kings*, 1961) and Ty Hardin (*PT 109*, 1963).

While we were visiting, a guy was going through the back rooms turning off all the lights. He seemed to be looking over the operations on the sound stage.

Then a historic moment happened. The guy finally came out, and to my amazement, he was none other than Jack Warner. He came up, greeted us personally, and shook our hands.

I was reminded of meeting Jack Warner when reading David Puttnam's *Movies and Money*. Puttnam said,

> "Jack Warner was ruthless in his quest to drive down costs. He would prowl around the studio late at night snapping off unnecessary lights to save money."

Jack Warner was one of a half dozen true studio czars who put the glamour into Hollywood. But it was 1963, a waning time for him and his studio, before he sold out and later became Warner Bros. Seven Arts.

Warner Bros. was now promoting a new crop of stars through a series of lower budget pictures. One of these

Two on a Guillotine (1965) promotional seminar with associates from Pacific Theatres at the Warner Bros. Studio. This movie was one of Jack Warner's efforts to promote new stars with lower budgeted pictures. Author on extreme right.

movies we saw at Warners was *Wall of Noise* (1963), starring Suzanne Pleshette, Ty Hardin and Dorothy Provine.

This attempt in a small way was reminiscent of what Jack Warner once did during their golden age with a prized stable of stars. Bette Davis, Joan Crawford, Errol Flynn, Edward G. Robinson, James Cagney, Humphrey Bogart and Paul Muni were big Warner names, but the studio was run by one man: Jack Warner.

We then moved into a luncheon meeting set up on another sound stage. It was elaborately decorated with the theme of Warners' new talent and their new release, *Spencer's Mountain*.

We came in from the bright sunlight to a darkened sound stage when I walked head-on into Dorothy Provine (*The Great Race*, 1965). She was more slender than she appeared on screen, so I was quite surprised when I found out who she was.

On another sound stage, we met several stars at a luncheon, including a couple Suzanne Pleshette (*The Birds*, 1963) and Troy Donahue (*A Summer Place*, 1959). They were married in 1964.

As a finale, Jack Warner formally introduced his new talent and his plans for a series of pictures to establish those new faces. The major picture that received the big push was *Spencer's Mountain*, starring Henry Fonda and Maureen O'Hara.

In retrospect, the biggest moment at Warner Bros. was meeting Jack Warner. At that time, he was the only living movie mogul still in control on a par with Samuel Goldywn, Harry Cohn, David Selznick, Darryll Zanuck, Adolph Zukor, and Louis B. Mayer.

FOREST WHITAKER (Bird, 1988)

[Parker was] the single most confident individual I've
ever seen in my life when he was playing the saxophone
... [after playing] He would just drift into the woodwork.
                    —*Clint Eastwood*

YOU CAN IMAGINE MY EXCITEMENT when Clint
Eastwood's publicist Marco Barla told me Forest Whitaker
was coming to Kansas City for the U.S. premiere of *Bird*,
based on the life of Kansas City's jazz saxophonist, Charlie
"Bird" Parker.

Forest had already won the award of Best Actor for *Bird*
at the 1987 Cannes Film Festival in France. The film
received the Grand Prize of the French Technical High
Commission for director Clint Eastwood's exceptional quality of sound track.

My office went into full swing to get the publicity campaign planned and rolling.

Upon his arrival, Forest Whitaker requested to visit the
grave of Charlie Parker. The next morning, on a misty
October day, we went in a town car to keep it low-keyed and
not to alert the press with a limo.

Still, a couple of television crews arrived just as he
walked up to the grave site at Lincoln Cemetery in
Independence, Missouri. It was a touching time for him, and
to hold the moment, he merely walked on down the hillside.

With Forest Whitaker and Ruby, at
the Ritz-Carlton Hotel before *Bird*
premiere at the Glenwood Theatre.

I believe that he approached the portrayal of "Bird" with deep, personal reverence. It seemed he had a spiritual experience, as though he was one with Parker. I'll never forget the moment as he, with his head bowed down, stood over the grave, truly a young man with deep personal conviction.

Later Forest talked about how personal it was for him to visit Charlie Parker's grave. Because Parker was a real person, Forest was committed to being honest and true to what "Bird" represented.

Eastwood's portrayal shows the great Charlie "Yardbird" Parker in the 'good ole' days of jazz. Parker was known for his role in the creation of be-bop jazz in the mid 1940's and was, incidentally, a real idol to the young Clint Eastwood.

Charlie Parker was born in Kansas City, Kansas, but his career began in Kansas City, Missouri. The movie traces Charlie Parker when he leaves Kansas City with Jay McShann and his band to make New York his new home. In New York, he created a new jazz under the influence of Thelonius Monk, Dizzy Gillespie, and others.

On the day of the red-carpet premiere, his personal publicist had to return to Beverly Hills; so she asked Ruby to fill in for her. Ruby and Forest arrived at the Glenwood Theatre with dozens of cameras flashing. Press came from all over the Midwest, even from Chicago. It was obvious *Bird* and Forest had magnetic star power.

This moment was captured in full color by *The Kansas City Star* the next morning with front-page coverage.

As we sat in the audience, waiting for the film to begin, a woman from behind got up and came over to ask for

Ruby with Forest Whitaker, after the premiere of *Bird* at the Charlie Parker Memorial Foundation ball in Overland Park, Kansas.

Forest's autograph. Ruby said he would be signing autographs after the screening. Then the woman used a choice word or two in response. It is a tough decision that a publicist has to make. One autograph would have demanded six-hundred more.

Then after the movie at 10 p.m., the Charlie Parker Memorial Foundation held a ball at the Overland Park Marriott Hotel. Eddie Baker, executive director of the foundation, performed with his big band, the New Breed Orchestra. K.C.'s Tap ambassadors, the McFadden Brothers, performed at the ball. The Parker Jazz Ensemble played for the reception. Press from across the country attended.

The premiere received an out-pouring of publicity. On September 26, Mayor Richard Berkley proclaimed Kansas City "Birdland" at a press conference. Eleven other surrounding cities announced similar proclamations to recognize the premiere.

In addition to his early love of Parker, Clint Eastwood said in an interview why he was drawn to do the movie, *Bird:*

> "Americans don't have any original art except western movies and jazz."

In researching *Bird*, Eastwood learned of Bruce Ricker, a New York attorney, who produced a Kansas City jazz film, *Last of the Blue Devils* (1979), a documentary about the reunion of Count Basie, Jay McShann and Big Joe Turner. At the suggestion of Warner Bros. vice president Joe Hyams, Clint sought out Ricker and purchased the French and Italian rights to *Last of the Blue Devils*. Eastwood released the film under his name in those countries to build his credentials as a jazz enthusiast before the release of *Bird*. The French loved the picture. All production costs were paid just from the revenue in France.

Ricker and Eastwood became movie jazz friends. Ricker, Eastwood, and Charlotte Zwerin produced Warner Bros. successful *Thelonious Monk: Straight, No Chaser* (1989).

Ricker came to Kansas City that year to promote *Thelonious Monk.*

Ricker also directed the PBS documentary *Clint Eastwood: Out of the Shadows* (2000), a film that surveys Clint's life.

Next see how the movie people support worthy causes with their talent.

FOUR

How The Movie People
Do Good Works

Every time a bell rings, an angel gets his wings.
—*Zuzu, It's a Wonderful Life*

I was thinking about should I change my movie? Should I change my life?
—*Woody Allen, Stardust Memories*

Creativity not committed to public purpose is merely therapy or ego satisfaction.
—*Ernest Jones*, advertising executive

I feel that the Superman role is one part in a series of parts I'll play over a lifetime.
—*Christopher Reeve*

Karolyn Grimes (Zuzu), reunited with Jimmy Stewart in 1990. Photo from *ZuZu's Wonderful Life in the Movies* by Christopher Brunell.

ON CHARITY PROJECTS, the movie people have been among the first to volunteer. Celebrities who have lent us a hand include Christopher Reeve, Jeff East, Rush Limbaugh, Buster Crabbe, Dennis James, Karolyn Grimes (Zuzu, *It's a Wonderful Life)*, Mark Harmon, Joe Kapp, Cheryl Jones, and Leon and Kersti Vitali (assistants to Stanley Kubrick).

"The Heart of Show Business" is the slogan of Variety Club International, one of the biggest movie-related charities. The movie industry has long been dedicated to worthy causes. I've continually been amazed at how generous the entertainment people are in giving back to the community. Helping out has always been another way the industry has touched its audience.

For example, Buster Crabbe ran a summer camp for boys near Saranac Lake, New York around the time he left Hollywood in the early 1950's. It was at the time he began a television career on WOR in New York with his *Buster's Buddies* show.

TEENS REACHING FOR THE STARS ...

Ruby and I created the non-profit Performing Arts Scholarship Foundation (1978) to give teenagers a positive influence in their lives.

We got the idea after being advisers for three years at the Unity World Headquarters with Youth of Unity.

We formed the performing arts "Star Reach," made up of youth entertainers. The purpose was to attract young people, ages 14-18, from the community at large. The guidelines were based on positive mental attitude, commitment to purpose, follow-through, and communication.

Right of author, Buster Crabbe (*Flash Gordon*), poet James Dillet Freeman (to left of bride) and our youth group at Unity World Headquarters, Lee's Summit, Missouri. Freeman wrote *I Am There*, the poem that was read from the moon in the summer of 1971 by Apollo 15 crew member, James B. Irwin.

The vehicle for these four skills was through entertaining seniors, children's hospital units, community and civic organizations as well as the Kansas City Missouri Summer Youth Program.

The mode of education was all-day workshops featuring mime, costume make-up, comedy skits, and dance. Drama teachers from Loretta Academy and Park College participated in the actual instruction and often became on-site helpers. Other leaders were parents of the young people or artists trained in the performing arts field.

On one occasion, 100 youths signed up for an all-day workshop at the Royals Stadium Club. A tap and jazz teacher came from Texas to help with the program.

On another occasion, Channel 9 newscaster and meteorologist Cheryl Jones made a personal appearance at one of the workshops on the Country Club Plaza. She later went on to CNN.

After a two-year involvement, performing in troupes monthly (some chose to participate weekly), the students who met the 4-Star guideline were eligible for scholarship nomination. They went on to various schools, such as the University of South Carolina, Southern Methodist University, University of Kansas, and Yale University.

One of the interesting concepts is that the youths all were responsible for helping to raise the funds. They did so through personal appearances at service organizations, the Kwanis Clubs, Variety Club, and group fundraisers, such as dance-a-thons at the Worlds of Fun amusement park.

The idea of Star Reach was three-fold: (1) to look for the star within, instead of the peer-pressure groups outside the individual. (2) to have a place to go that gave back to the community, and (3) to help youth develop a real presence through personal growth within healthy groups their own age.

These young people loved performing for children's hospitals, especially when they could wear costumes that entertained the children, such as those from *Pippi Longstocking*

Star Reach performers at a care center in the Kansas City area.
(Left bottom photo) Fund-raising at Worlds of Fun.

in the South Seas (1974) or Clyde the orangutan to the Clint Eastwood picture *Any Which Way But Loose (1978).* Teen enthusiasm was contagious. Residents soon forgot their ills and aches amid the youths' smiles and friendliness.

SUPERMAN LENDS A HAND

Celebrities pitched in to help. Christopher Reeve, from *Superman, the Movie,* signed a poster for the Star Reach group. This gift, with its encouraging message, stimulated these young teens. Dennis James and Kansas City's Jeff East, did public service announcements for Star Reach.

Live appearance of characters from the movie, *Pippi Longstocking in the South Seas* (1974) along with the Star Reach Performers at Children's Mercy Hospital in Kansas City.

Jeff East, who played Superman as a boy in the Reeve film, taped the following television spot for use on Channel 41 in Kansas City:

(*Superman, the Movie* theme up and under):
Hi! Jeff East.
I wish there had been Star Reach Seminars
when I began my career as a teen-ager.
Youth 14-18 learn creative drama, jazz,
disco, contemporary dance, aerobics, and
stage make-up for costuming. Learn
to better communicate with others through
Star Reach: youth performers reaching
people who need people.

Rush Limbaugh also did an informative Q & A video with both Ruby and me on "Star Reach" at Channel 41 TV.

TEENS LEARN INTERVIEW SKILLS

Another new skill the teens learned was how to conduct celebrity interviews. A couple of the interviews were Carl Weathers, *Rocky II* (1979), and Joe Kapp, former Minnesota Viking quarterback for the movie, *Over the Edge* (1979).

What the program taught us is that the young people are very energetic and enthusiastic, once they have direction and focus. There is often much talent just ready to come forth with a little guidance.

A CHRISTMAS TIME WITH ZUZU

Karolyn Grimes (Zuzu in *It's a Wonderful Life*), has given us fund-raising support for the Indian Missionary Society to help their missions and to bring needed Catholic priests from India to the United States. Zuzu has also helped to raise money for restoration of the historic St. Mary's in Kansas City. This connection was natural with Zuzu's famous line from *It's A Wonderful Life:*

"Every time a bell rings, an angel gets his wings."

St. Mary's historic Episcopal Church has 405 bells, the largest carillon system of its kind in any church in the world, according to its music director, Dr. Bruce Prince-Joseph.

In a December, 1994 interview at our home with Dr. Douglas Moore of Fox TV's News in Kansas City, Zuzu tells why *It's A Wonderful Life* is so important in viewers' lives:

"I think the impact it has had on the American people is so big because they all can identify with it, certainly some part of it.

"A lot of dreams have never been fulfilled, and George Bailey's certainly were not fulfilled in the movie. But yet, in retrospect, he had a chance to look at his life and he could see they were not the right dreams; so we can all do the same thing.

"I also think that people sometimes feel that they wish they had not been born. I think the movie reassures them to know that it is a normal feeling and very pertinent to trying to get through times today. So viewers benefit from that principle.

"I think it is the number-one movie because the American people have put it into their hearts. It's an American film as compared to the British *A Christmas Carol. It's A Wonderful Life* is the quintessential American movie.

"Frank Capra, the director, was one of the greats and will always be considered one of the greats of our time. His influence made the film what it is because of the man he was. He could make things work.

"Recently I designed a lovely 15" doll representing the young Zuzu from the movie. It has become a wonderful collectible.

"The Target stores sent us on a world promotion for the Zuzu doll. They reunited the Bailey family kids from the movie. And then Jimmy Stewart's hometown of Indiana, Pennsylvania decided to do a special thing: They reunited the whole cast in a very special reunion."

Such were the comments of Karolyn Grimes, one of the special stars who helped us in charity endeavors. We feel honored to have worked with stars together as a way of giving back to the community as well as helping young people get a more solid footing for the future.

An interesting parallel between our charity work and the story of *It's a Wonderful Life* arises in George Bailey's receiving "the greatest gift" of being able to see the world around him without his influence on it. What he did in life, and what we do for others, often goes unnoticed; yet it has an amazing positive effect.

During World War I, actress Marie Dressler was active in raising money for Liberty Bonds. She gave a new twist to an old cliché. She said, "Don't give till it hurts. Give till you feel a nice rosy glow." As George Bailey knew, and as we all must learn, that sentiment is the essence of true charity.

In the next two chapters, read the stories on how publicity stunts are done to promote movie comedies and movie dramas.

FIVE

How Humor Entices You
To The Box Office

Manigator, Alliman…Seagator, Gatorgal—Galligator!
—John Goodman as schlock horror movie producer getting
ideas as he looks at a stuffed alligator, *Matinee* (1993)

Humor is the shortest distance between two people.
—*Victor Borge*

It's a funny world—a man's lucky if he gets out of it alive.
—*W. C. Fields*, *You're Telling Me* (1934)

One horse-laugh is worth ten thousand syllogisms. It is not only more
effective; it is vastly more intelligent.
—*H. L. Mencken*

All the really good ideas I ever
had came to me while I was
milking a cow.
—*Grant Wood*

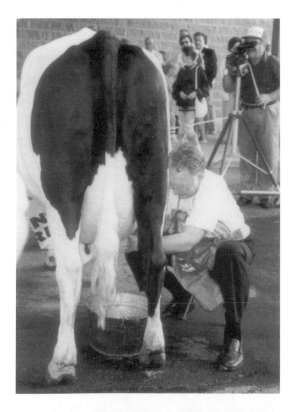

He who laughs, lasts.
—*Mary Pettibone Poole*

In Kansas City, George Burns gets
clipped by Gracie Allen between live
stage performances. Burns reminisced
about those early Kansas City days at
our Oh God! (1977) publicity meeting
at the Warner Bros. studio.

Celebrity Cow-Milking
publicity stunt for *Funny Farm*,
in parking lot of Bannister
Square theatres, with NBC's Dr.
Doug Moore getting into action.

PROMOTION IS A DIRECT APPEAL to the eyes and ears of moviegoers to gain their involvement. It fits into the earlier non-traditional definition of Hollywood:

It's a place of escape, where you fulfill the drama (and humor) needed in your daily life.

Exploitation is at the core of Hollywood. Because producers make movies that exploit the dreams and desires of the movie-going public. Films from Hollywood reflect what the public demands.

A publicist presents a movie as something dramatically different from other movies playing. The attributes of the film are built into appeals that are marketable.

Humor has been a key element to many successful publicity campaigns. This tactic is used not only for comedies but also for other films that lend themselves to exploitation.

Humor often can present a movie the best possible light. A publicist has to maintain a positive attitude to be successful selling movies to the public. Often publicists have to discount their own tastes when promoting a film.

We use humor to create news through publicity stunts. It's not really news happening by itself—it's creating news!

Movie publicists give these stunts a sense of spirit that can appear extravagant and sometimes outlandish. Such creativity can achieve tremendous exposure for a movie and the stars.

The ideas that emerged from studio meetings were unusual and became even more entertaining through the creative personalities behind them. Stars, producers, directors, and product tie-in managers enlivened our meetings.

ALMIGHTY LAUGHS

George Burns, before *Oh God* (1977) had its debut, came to the Warner Bros. studio meeting and entertained the publicists for more than half an hour. Carl Reiner was also there to motivate us on the promotion of the film. Burns did mention Kansas City. He reminisced about his appearances at the old Orpheum Theatre next to the Muehlebach Hotel.

These meetings worked like a creative master-mind group, using the experiences and thought-power from many different areas of the country.

THE FIRST CERTIFIED CRAZY PERSON'S COMEDY

At our studio meetings, we became a part of Hollywood screenings and events. In 1979, we attended the first showing of the outrageous comedy *The In-Laws* starring Peter Falk and Alan Arkin. It took place at the Director's Theatre on Sunset Boulevard in Hollywood. We were seeing it with an audience months in advance to generate publicity ideas for the next day's meeting. It was a way to get first-hand input on the reactions of the audience.

Many Hollywood stars were at the theater, including Peter Falk and Rudolph Neurehev.

After the movie, we walked into a lavish reception catered by Hollywood's famous Chasen's of Beverly Hills. This informal setting allowed the publicists time to gain further input from members of the audience.

A GREAT IDEA BORN INSTANTLY

Warner Bros. legendary publicist, Marty Weiser, was always quietly working behind the scenes. I was always surprised by the great ideas that just popped into Marty's head. One time, he and I were in a small meeting of maybe eight publicists. He leaned over to show me a sketch of a premiere ticket. It was to be a screening pass in the shape of a policeman's badge for the comedy *Police Academy* (1984). That was the instant the idea was born, right next to me, and it went into national use.

NEVER GIVE A SAGA AN EVEN BREAK

Marty had what many referred to as the "Weiser Touch." One of his funniest promotions ever was for Mel Brooks' *Blazing Saddles* (1974). He said:

> "*Blazing Saddles* needed something outrageous. I invited horses and their friends to a special drive-in showing at the Pickwick Drive-in in L.A. I chose it because of the proximity to Griffith Park, surrounded by stables. Soon 250 horses showed up, and their owners lined them up where cars usually parked.

> "We had a hospitality bar. For the horses we served oats in popcorn buckets and had a lot of fun with it. We had a laughing horse. If you touched it in a certain place, it gave a horse laugh. All three networks—NBC, CBS, and ABC —came out and put it on the network news.

> "It was humorous. That's pure exploitation and again, the best exploitation is based on humor."

PRESS CARRIED AWAY TO THE FUNNY FARM

Another humorous stunt was an "udderly" ridiculous Celebrity Cow-Milking contest for a Chevy Chase comedy *Funny Farm* (1988). We did it in Kansas City and throughout our territory that included Wichita, Omaha, and Des Moines. *Funny Farm* is about Chevy Chase and his wife's dreams of an idyllic, rural utopia away from New York's mean streets, but those dreams are comically shattered when a farmer's exalted fantasies do not become a Norman Rockwell image.

Part of the strategy was to invite the Kansas City and regional media to a cow-milking contest held adjacent to the Bannister Square theatres.

Then Zarda Dairy got involved in our radio promotion and stunt activities.

We planted a giant Zarda Dairy cow in the theatre parking lot to give the promotion larger-than-life drama. Dr. Doug Moore with WDAF TV was taped milking a cow. Each press representative was fitted with an apron and a minimum of instruction as the fun began. Even an Elvis lookalike joined in. Media coverage included NBC, CBS, Time Warner Cable and several print outlets.

A comedy from Chevy Chase was the original *National Lampoon Vacation* (1983). A great idea came out of that promotion. We held the national press junket down in the Grand Canyon, a highlight vacation spot in the story, where the studio actually made the movie. The press loved it, and the idea netted great exposure. It's a fine example of using a locale to add meaning through exploitation.

DIVE-IN AT THE MOVIES

We created interest for a new Warner Bros. comedy by selecting an unusual location for a premiere.

I wondered about choosing a completely different venue. We tied in a radio-station sponsor for on-air coverage and planned, for the very first time anywhere, an advance premiere at an amusement water park, Oceans of Fun in Kansas City, Missouri.

"Dive-In at the movies" was the theme. It was a premiere location for *Young Einstein* (1988), starring Australian cult star Yahoo Serious. It was perfect for this movie that could be viewed like a music video, surrounded by water pranks, and bikinis.

At the Hollywood lab that built No. 5 during the studio publicity meeting for *Short Circuit II* (1988).

NUTS AND BOLTS CAN BE FUNNY

Publicity for a humorous picture can be based on technology such as for Tri-Star's *Short Circuit 2* (1988).

Ruby and I attended publicity meetings on the picture in Los Angeles and visited the research labs where the film's robot, "No. 5" was produced. Then the robot was demonstrated to generate publicity ideas.

As an added touch, the publicists were invited guests at the

Beverly Hills home of David Jones, producer of *Short Circuit 2*.

Back in Kansas City, we built our promotion around a family festival at Hallmark's Crown Center shopping center with hayrides, games, and a cowboy on stilts. *Short Circuit 2* got a world of light-hearted, humorous exposure through this event. Also Hallmark gave the picture a lot of exposure through their in-house media outlets.

STAGED HUMOR WITH *THE PRIZE FIGHTER*

A press conference with a star and a locally staged tie-in can be a news-maker in itself. Here is the copy from a pictorial news release we used for the Tim Conway screwball comedy, *The Prize Fighter* (1979):

> "Tim Conway, motion picture and television star to millions with his unparalleled comedic genius, hopes to tell about his new role in a press conference staged for Tuesday, December 18, at the Italian Gardens Restaurant, 1110 Baltimore.

> "The 1:30 p.m. conference will find Mr. Conway committing his personal lifestyle to a newly-found macho image he so naturally portrays in *The Prize Fighter,* a New World Pictures film distributed by John Shipp, co-starring Don Knotts.

> *"The Prize Fighter* will no doubt vault Conway into the elite 'sex symbol' category as female audiences swoon at the muscular visage of 'ter-

Ruby and Dan Meyers with No. 5 at the Beverly Hills
home of David Foster, producer of *Short Circuit II*.

rible Tim' in the boxing ring. Conway expects to
bolster this macho image in Kansas City with a
challenge going to famed area boxer Tony
Chiaverini, current holder of the United States
Boxing Association Junior Middleweight title.
Chiaverini will be on hand to deflate all threats,
making certain this will be Conway's final challenge.

"Joe Serviss, Mayor Pro Tem of Kansas City,
will present Conway with a key to the city. It is
hopeful the ceremony will occur early in the press

conference, prior to Conway's confrontation with
Tony Chiaverini for obvious health reasons."

It turned out the 'fight' was not more than "shadow boxing." Though both men emerged unscathed, the effect was
superb.

A NUDIST'S EYE VIEW

We never knew exactly where we'd find exposure or
how it would happen. Sometimes we were prepared for it,
sometimes not. It's the resulting benefit that counts.

For example, this is the way one story went based on a
taped interview with Marty Weiser in 1987.

Marty went to Denver for the Warner Bros. picture called
The Girl From Jones Beach (1949), starring Ronald Reagan
as a magazine-cover artist and the glamorous blonde beauty Virginia Mayo.

Marty found that the hotel where he normally stayed
was booked up, and he asked, "Why?"

He discovered the Nudists of America were having their
national convention there, and Marty thought:

> "I recalled about a month previously, Virginia
> Mayo was at the beach at Malibu, and we had a
> photographer there for one of our stunts. The
> waves were very rough, so she lost the upper part
> of her bathing suit and immediately covered up
> with a towel."

"Snap!" "Snap!" The photographer wasted no time, but I must say, the release photo was in very good taste, and it got national distribution immediately.

Marty sought out the publicity director for the Nudists' convention. Marty suggested to him what he thought was a very good idea:

> "Because Virginia Mayo was momentarily a 'semi-nudist' a month ago—because of the AP Wire Photo—that perhaps the convention could honor her."

Marty wrote a story based on the idea for the publicity director to present to the convention. He wasn't sure they would pass such a resolution, but thought:

> "Virginia Mayo, selected 'the best undressed nudist of the year' or 'the best undressed actress of the year' had a chance of making it to newspapers."

The nudists thought it was a great stunt and they approved.

Marty went to the *Denver Post* managing editor with the story. However, what he didn't count on was that instead of the use of Virginia Mayo in a bathing suit, they took another picture of a nudist holding the original picture of startled Virginia with her emergency towel at Malibu. The caption told about the honor that she just received from the Nudist Association as the Best Undressed Actress of the Year.

It broke on the front page of the *Denver Post* and was picked up by United Press.

But alas! Marty was fired by one of his bosses. The boss exclaimed:

> "Don't you realize this girl is a member of the church choir and a very upright citizen? Her name being associated with nudists is contrary to her way of life. She is very, very unhappy about this and she went to Jack Warner with it and wants to break her contract. Nothing but trouble. So you're through. Pack up and get off the lot."

Thirty minutes later, his bigger boss called and said:

> "You're not fired. In fact, I'm calling you to tell you what a great stunt it was."

Marty felt very guilty about this, because he knew Virginia Mayo was a very nice person. He came up with the following idea:

> "Why don't I write a story to send to the papers that Virginia Mayo, upon receiving the honor from the Nudist Association in Denver as the Best Undressed Actress of the Year, says 'No, Thank You.' She would rather be known as the best <u>dressed</u> actress. She has 469 dresses, and 675 hats and all kinds of shoes. I made quite an impressive list. I felt that's a good story, 'She says, No thanks' to the award."

Marty wrote the above press release immediately when he got to the studio. It broke bigger than the first story. That meant a picture of Virginia Mayo in a bathing suit in *Time* magazine with the "No, Thanks" story. Everywhere the first story broke, this story broke. Now it was really news, because she said: "No, Thanks" to some honor. She wanted to be known as the "best dressed," not the "best dressed undressed." She thanked Marty for it later.

HUMOROUS EXPOSURE
FROM RUSH LIMBAUGH COUNTS

Rush had a good time with the movie *Purple Rain* (1984) starring Prince. He put together a one-minute skit with the sound bites that aired on KMBZ radio.

He used it throughout the program for two or three days on KMBZ. We couldn't have bought this kind of exposure. Prince's fans made it a big hit in Kansas City and elsewhere. Sometimes humorous controversy creates great, though unintended interest in a movie!

DO "THE SWARM"

Months before the release of Irwin Allen's *The Swarm* (1978), these were the publicity headlines that warned of the picture's arrival:

Swarm of Killer Bees Terrorizes South Texas
- Air Force Missile Complex Neutralized by Lethal Bees!
- Scores Die in Silos!
- Command Stymied by Attack!
- Helicopters Downed!

Irwin Allen produced such boxoffice hits as *The Poseidon Adventure* (1972), and *The Towering Inferno* (1974). We and other publicists from around the country came to the studio to get a first-hand briefing from Mr. Allen.

We had heard how demanding Irwin Allen could be; so meeting him was an awesome experience. Some executives at Warner Bros. seemed to be more afraid of Mr. Allen than of his killer bees. One studio executive gave a report to our meeting, and Mr. Allen immediately got up and barked at him:

"Take a cut in pay!"

BILLIONS OF KILLER BEES

Mr. Allen spoke to us about the background of *The Swarm*. He saw *The Swarm* as a prophecy of what was coming to the U.S. from Central America.

Allen said *The Swarm* was a story of survival, of towns and residents against the most deadly enemy of all: killer bees. The movie portrayed the death and destruction that soon would overwhelm the Texas gulf and Southwestern states before the century was out.

Many laughed. But Irwin's premise, to a lesser degree, came true.

Allen offered publicists a large bonus as a prize to develop the most creative strategies for selling the picture to the public.

A LIGHTER TOUCH FOR THE SWARM

To be successful we needed to find a lighter, humorous approach to selling *The Swarm*, instead of the gloom and doom of the advertising campaign.

KBEQ - FLYING CIRCUS DISCO PRESENTS

SWARM NIGHT

SATURDAY JULY 8TH
AT
WORLDS OF FUN
4545 WORLDS OF FUN AVENUE KANSAS CITY, MISSOURI
AND INTRODUCES THE LATEST IN DISCO
"THE SWARM"
EXCLUSIVE FOR IRWIN ALLEN'S PRODUCTION OF "THE SWARM"
NATIONWIDE RELEASE JULY 14TH

"COCA-COLA SWARM"
DISCO DANCE INSTRUCTIONS

(1) *TAP-STEP TO THE LEFT (COUNT 1 - 2) HIP MOVES OVER SIDE STEP BEFORE SHOULDERS (CREATING A SWAY)

TAP-STEP TO THE RIGHT (COUNT 1 - 2) USING SAME STYLE AS ABOVE.

(2) WITH FEET APART - SWAY LEFT - RIGHT (COUNT 1 - 2)

(3) QUICK FORWARD WITH LEFT FOOT TOGETHER WITH RIGHT (TAP) (COUNT & 1)

QUICK BACK WITH RIGHT FOOT TOGETHER WITH LEFT FOOT (TAP) (COUNT & 2)

(AS FEET MOVE FORWARD HANDS GO BEHIND BACK - AS FEET MOVE BACK HANDS GO IN FRONT OF BODY)

*TAP HAS NO WEIGHT ON FOOT
STEP HAS WEIGHT ON FOOT

(4) WITH FEET TOGETHER MAKE CIRCULAR ACTION WITH HIPS AND LEFT HAND OVER HEAD (CREATING A SWARM) (COUNT 1 - 2)

(5) QUICK BACK WITH LEFT FOOT TOGETHER WITH RIGHT FOOT (TAP)* COUNT & 1)
QUICK FORWARD WITH RIGHT FOOT

TOGETHER WITH LEFT FOOT (TAP)* (COUNT & 2)

(HAND STYLING REVERSES WITH BODY MOVEMENT AS ABOVE)

THE FIRST HALF CAN BE REPEATED AS MANY TIMES AS NEEDED TO MAKE A COMPLETE TURN BEFORE GOING FORWARD AND BACK INTO THE

"COCA COLA SWARM"

DISCO CONTEST PRIZES

Our core promotion was a new disco type dance called "The Swarm." Ruby and Vera Haire—both choreographers —developed the dance from scratch and demonstrated it on Kansas City news television programs. We presented "The Swarm" (the dance) live, publicly for the first time at the Signboard Club located in Hallmark's Crown Center Hotel.

When Warner Bros. studio publicity coordinator, Leo Wilder, called me about the idea, he said Irwin Allen and the Warner Bros. executives loved it.

We sold the idea to KBEQ-FM radio, Coca Cola Co., and Worlds of Fun amusement park to co-operate in the pro-motion. All three promotional partners were enthusiastic about it.

Coke attached "The Swarm" dance instructions on their store products prior to "Swarm Night" at Worlds of Fun. This gimmick enabled participants to learn "The Swarm" dance before an upcoming contest at the Flying Disco at Worlds of Fun.

KBEQ ran dozens of pre-promotional spots blanketing the Kansas City target audience.

MORE BUZZ ON THE SWARM

As word-of-mouth spread regionally, the contest grew larger. Other stations wanted to get on board in "The Swarm" contest. Disc jockeys built great public interest in Des Moines, Omaha, Wichita, Topeka, St. Joseph, and Springfield, and many other cities.

In addition, KBEQ ran a "Mystery Bee" contest. The Mystery Bee was a local celebrity. The disc jockey invited

Forty thousands flyers promoted SWARM NIGHT at Worlds of Fun and convenience stores, when we introduced our new disco dance, "The Swarm."

listeners to call KBEQ after each on-air clue. They recorded the first caller's guess along with the name and address and they announced the winner on July 8th at "Swarm Night" at Worlds of Fun.

Further, KBEQ ran 30-second "scenarios" that could come true based on facts about killer bees. The idea was to boost awareness of the factual background of *The Swarm*.

WHB Radio also got involved. That added to the depth of the promotion. WHB announced that the WHBeekeeper would be stationed at several Kansas City shopping centers the weekend of July 1st. Its disc jockey would be dressed in a bee-keeper costume and would be asking listeners to approach the DJ at different shopping centers. The station announcer told listeners to use a certain pre-announced phrase such as "Bee my Honey," to win The Swarm T-shirts, and passes.

At the big finale, judges picked a final winner based on the ability to perform *The Swarm* disco dance learned from the instructions we gave out plus any new movements a dancer could create individually. The winner received His and Her Motorcycles choosing from Kawasaki, Honda, or Suzuki.

The final touch came when the Dan Meyers agency received a top national prize.

Publicity Stunts

Out for all the fun that money can buy! An "Arthur Car" promotes the Dudley Moore's Best Actor role in *Arthur* (1981).

Costume promotion for the last Peter Sellers movie, *The Fiendish Plot of Dr. FuManchu* (1980).

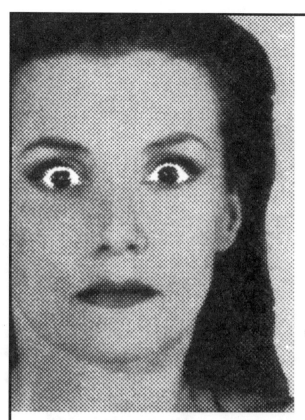

From Henri-
Georges Clouzot
–France's Master
of Suspense

... IT WILL MAKE
YOUR EYEBALLS *Pop!*

"DIABOLIQUE"

STARRING

SIMONE SIGNORET · VERA CLOUZOT · PAUL MEURISSE
Produced by Filmsonor, Paris · Released by UMPO, Inc.

<u>IMPORTANT:</u> During the entire engage-
ment no one will be admitted into the theatre once
the main feature has begun. Please observe the
following Feature Time Schedule carefully.

FEATURE: 12:00, 2:00, 4:00, 6:00, 8:00, 10:00

DON'T REVEAL THE ENDING!

New York viewing policy ad for *Diabolique* (1955). The film was marketed
as a publicity commodity that predates Hitchcock's *Psycho* (1960)

SIX

How Drama Draws You
To The Movies

If you take the average fairground midway, you find people paying money to be frightened—the haunted house, for example, where the floorboards move up and down, skeletons pop up, spiders drop down—and it's all done on the basis of humor.
—*Alfred Hitchcock*

If there is no excitement ready-made, some must be manufactured.
—*Silas Bent, Ballyhoo*

Nothing draws a crowd like a crowd.
—*P. T. Barnum*

Hey, Woolsey, the crowd is turning into a mob! Congratulations!
—Theatre mogul to *John Goodman, Matinee*

Author under a banner at Warner Bros. publicity meeting for *The Exorcist*.

VARIETY MAGAZINE ANNOUNCES that theatre owners tell tales of patrons fainting while seeing *The Blair Witch Project* (1999) and that fans have had recurring nightmares and insomnia from seeing the film.

Movie titles can be suggestive of a "hoax," a humorous or mischievous deception to generate publicity. *The Blair Witch Project* was a fictional docu-drama made to seem "real."

This situation reminded me of what seemed a hoax surrounding the Warner Bros. publicity meeting for *The Exorcist (1973)*. Warner Bros. publicity department announced to us that they could not show the film because the production equipment at the studio suddenly stopped working. The implication was that the Devil was behind it. It seemed like a great way to get us to buy into the publicity.

Marty Weiser at Warner Bros. reported to the press that someone fainted while leaving a showing of *The Exorcist*. Then he planned a press showing with nurses and ambulances in attendance. It sounds a little like what happened on *The Blair Witch Project*.

One thing for certain about *The Blair Witch Project*, it was a revival of early movie showmanship. What's more, its entire (nearly) marketing campaign was conducted via the relatively new Internet. The public bought into the campaign that became a commodity.

This low-budget movie turned the studio mind-set upside down. How could a small distributor like Artisan use the Internet to generate so much publicity? Should studios start producing similar low-budget films? Are all the millions of dollars that studios spend merely a waste? Will Internet promotions revolutionize the industry?

In my opinion, Artisan engaged in what studios used to do: risk-taking. Its boldness in using a realistic story approach on a website about a year in advance was making use of the Internet, but the rest of it was just old-time show-manship which many in Hollywood have never seen or have forgotten.

EXPLOITATION WORKS ON HIGH-CLASS DRAMAS

For movie dramas "exploitation" is done through the use of public relations and advertising techniques to promote a star, movie, or product.

David O. Selznick flew the entire population of Zenda, (Ontario, Canada), to New York's Radio City Music Hall for the world premiere of *The Prisoner of Zenda (1937)*. The town's population was a total of fifty proud citizens. That's just one simple, but clever example of exploitation applied to a highly dramatic movie.

PUBLICITY CAN EXPLOIT THE NEWS

A publicist should relate the campaign so that the film's release ties in to hard news. Take, for instance, Paramount's *Another Time, Another Place* (1958), released to take advan-tage of the publicity surrounding the affair of Lana Turner and gangster boyfriend Johnny Stompanato.

First, Stompanato threatens Sean Connery with a gun over Lana Turner. Then Connery responds by decking

Stompanato. Later back in the U.S., Lana Turner's teenage daughter stabs Stompanato to death.

As late as 1997, the sensation of this scandalous Hollywood news of Lana Turner and Johnny Stompanato was again surfacing in the crime noir plot of *L.A. Confidential.*

A BOOK TITLE OFFERS
AN EXPLOITATION OPPORTUNITY

On a family picture called *A Little Princess* (1995), we used the movie's title to advantage. The publicity utilized advertising in *The Kansas City Star* before the event, and then follow-up publicity afterward.

The Kansas City Star became the sponsor and invited readers to the movie. Warner Bros. provided the theatre and the use of the film.

The *Kansas City Star's* first ad invited children as guests to the movie and then asked all to pose for a group picture. The copy read: "Come dressed as a little prince or princess. A group picture of all participants will be taken after the premiere." A follow-up publicity ad ran the next week, showing the group photo and reporting on the success of the event. It was a very simple promotion, but very effective for a movie based on a widely-known novel.

WARNER BROS. EXPLOITS NEW 3-D TECHNOLOGY

Warner Bros. used varying technologies to publicity advantage, first in 1927 with the new talkies (sound movies), and in the early fifties by releasing two fine quality 3-D movies. The first 3-D movies were quickie low-budget exploitation films, but in 1953, Warner Bros. released *The House of Wax* (1953), starring Vincent Price, the first 3-D feature made by a major studio. Warner Bros. produced *Dial M For Murder* (1954), starring James Stewart and Grace Kelly. That film took full advantage of the 3-D effects through the talents of Alfred Hitchcock. Both films were successful, but the expensive and complex technology precluded further releases in the 3-D format.

ALFRED HITCHCOCK: IT'S ONLY A MOVIE ...

Alfred Hitchcock was a master of suspense and also a master at building himself to star status as a director. All that a film company had to mention was that it was a Hitchcock film, and theatres booked it. His 1960 release campaign for *Psycho* (1960) showed his genius for creating value through self-promotion of his persona.

He used the newspaper ads to publicize his promotional plan. In addition, there were advance in-theater posters and a lobby phonograph record that announced his strict policy for admittance to see *Psycho*. Ads and other materials used the following copy to underscore his enforced viewing policies:

> "No one ... BUT NO ONE ... will be admitted to the theatre after the start of each performance of *PSYCHO*.

> "This is to help you enjoy *PSYCHO* more. By the way, after you see the picture, please don't give away the ending. It's the only one we have."

Theatres were held strictly to Hitchcock's policy. They actually turned patrons away which caused more comment and built a further desire to want to see *Psycho*. This campaign generated considerable word-of-mouth advertising and is a good example of what we call a "whisper" campaign. I whisper to you, and you pass it on.

EXPLOITATION THROUGH ADVERTISING

Hitchcock's persona gave a thrust of powerful believability to the viewing of *Psycho*.

What many don't know is that Hitchcock's promotional format had a forerunner five years earlier on a French film: Henri-Georges Clouzot's *Les Diabolique* (1955). It utilized one of the most effective publicity campaigns ever for a movie through the use of paid newspaper advertising.

The unprecedented publicity presentation consisted of five steps. It was made an integral part of the contract between the film distributor and theater owner. These were the actual theatrical exhibition guidelines:

1. DON'T REVEAL THE ENDING!

Because of the extraordinary nature of *Diabolique*, it is vital that all promotion and advertising material stress the line:

"Don't Reveal the Ending."

This request applied firmly to the press as well as to the public. It made the press an implied partner in keeping the secret. Publicity cast and credits carried the following line:

"The film that you are about to see is *DIABOLIQUE*, (first released in France as Les Diaboliques), an extraordinary new motion picture produced and directed by Henri-Georges Clouzot, France's master of suspense. It received the French motion picture Critics' Award, The Dellue Critics' Prize, and probably is the most talked-about film on the continent today.

And, may we ask you, please ... Let's keep the ending between us!"

In order to impress upon the public the importance of not revealing the ending of *Diabolique*, the theatres issued a copy of a Contract of Agreement with each ticket. This contract created tremendous talk in the industry and was a good publicity device because the patrons took copies home and distributed them to friends.

2. CONTRACT OF AGREEMENT

" With the purchase of this ticket, I do hereby agree that I, the party of the first part, in consideration of the fullest enjoyment of the film by other parties, will not by my own free will or under duress, directly or indirectly, reveal the ending of Henri-Georges Clouzot's *DIABOLIQUE* to my relatives, friends, or even enemies."

Signed by ....

3. "CLOSED DOOR" POLICY

This term identifies the policy, established during the New York showing, that no one will be seated in the theatre once the feature has begun. Advertising and promotion material must include the following statement:

"NO ONE WILL BE SEATED IN THE THEATRE ONCE THE MAIN FEATURE HAS STARTED.

PLEASE WATCH THE FEATURE SCHEDULE."

This policy also applied to the press, and the following request was made in connection with all screening notices:

"NOTE: We earnestly request you to be prompt, for the doors of the screening room will be closed after the film has started!"

LINES OUTSIDE THE THEATRE

Theater managers were told in campaign planning:

"You will discover that after the first day, patrons begin to arrive at the theatre for each showing, so that starting about 20 minutes before the feature goes on, lines will form outside. These lines, far from acting as an irritant, have actually been responsible for creating talk and enthusiasm around town for *DIABOLIQUE*, because every showman knows lines spell a hit and everyone is eager to get down to the theatre and to see what goes on."

PRESS RELEASES on these two unprecedented methods of presentation—(1) The Closed Door Policy and (2) Contract of Agreement—were sent out in connection with the opening of *Diabolique.*

From the above campaign material on *Diabolique*, five years earlier than *Psycho*, the reader will notice that Hitchcock's campaign was not unique with him. Hitchcock may have been inspired by this French promotion, and wisely re-applied it in 1960.

Again, Hitchcock used his image for a publicity photo opportunity to promote *Frenzy* (1972). He floated a dummy of himself down the Thames river in England.

WILLIAM CASTLE—MASTER OF HORROR GIMMICKS

During the 1950's, producer William Castle made several exploitation horror films that were merchandised through gimmicks. *Macabre*, *The House on Haunted Hill* (1958), and *The Tingler* (1959) were successful examples.

Castle used a variety of publicity devices such as "Death by Fright" insurance, floating glow-in-the-dark skeletons above the audience and seats wired to give shocks to patrons during certain scenes. The gimmicks fooled willing audiences, and they loved it. It proved to me that audiences enjoy being "put on" by gimmicks.

WARNER BROS. EXHIBITOR SEMINAR IN KANSAS CITY— for the twin bill *Dracula A.D.1972* and *Crescendo*. Among those pictured are, left to right: James Beauchamp, Floyd Brethour, Don Young, Jack Poessiger, Martin Stone, Michelle Sands, the author and Jess Spain.

RUSH LIMBAUGH'S NIGHT IN A HAUNTED HOUSE

One of my enjoyable times with Rush was in 1976 when we were to spend a night, as a radio promotion, with a group of psychics in a haunted house in the Hyde Park area of Kansas City.

It was a promotion for the United Artists release of *Burnt Offerings* (1976). The story is about a family who move into a haunted house in the country.

The location of the promotion was in an old neighborhood that lent itself to the movie theme of hauntings.

The idea was for Rush to spend a night in the haunted house and report live to his audience the next morning on disco radio KUDL-FM. He announced on-air that he would later report the strange things that went on during that night.

When Rush and I approached the house with the rustle of October leaves at our feet, low-glowing orange light emanated from windows of the three-story house.

We could see that members of the Kansas City Psychical Research Society were already inside investigating the hauntings.

SPOOK CHASERS

Once inside, spook lights immediately started blinking all over the place. This was to be a sign that there was spirit activity. The psychics told us that cold spots are areas spirits like to frequent.

Rush listened, but couldn't resist laughing out loud.

The two gentlemen who lived in the house told Rush and me tales of being awakened at all times during the night by an old man with long, white hair. He seemed to constantly whisper in their ears.

Rush saw a lot of humor in the situation and expressed his views. Then one of them told me that Rush had to leave, because the spirits didn't like his attitude.

So we quietly left, but Rush surely had a great time describing the event to his radio audience the next morning. United Artists got a lot of exposure for *Burnt Offerings*.

PUBLICIST ESCAPES FROM K.C. THROUGH EXPLOITATION PLAN

Famed Warner Bros. publicist Marty Weiser, after a two-year stint in Kansas City, wanted to be transferred back to the Burbank studio. He was afraid it would never happen because he had been complimented so much for his work in the Midwest.

Feeling frustrated, he stayed up most of one night to dream up a stunt on *They Drive By Night* (1940) that would get him back to the Warner Bros. Studio. It was a story of Humphrey Bogart as a trucker, and of his friend, George Raft, and the waitresses they met on these overnight truck trips: Ann Sheridan and Ida Lupino.

Marty then made arrangements for the Teamsters to select Ann Sheridan as "The girl they would most like to give a lift to." This story broke on the AP and UPI wire services.

His studio boss insisted that Marty start the tour from Chicago and he did.

Marty befriended famed D-Day photographer Burt Brant from Kansas City, and they flew ahead to each town to chronicle the stunt in progress. Brant would take the pictures to the local Acme Bureau and then wired them throughout the country. Dozens of photo breaks in newspapers resulted.

In each city, they went to the mayor's office or governor's office in state capitols to have them autograph the side of the truck.

Then a big break came when presidential candidate Wendell L. Willkie and the governor of Colorado autographed the truck in Colorado Springs. This story broke front page in New York City and in papers throughout the country.

Marty pulled an added stunt on *They Drive By Night*. He drove a truck up in front of *The Kansas City Star* building. Inside the truck, he had sawdust on the floor and a little bar with pictures of Ann Sheridan on the walls, and the entire *Star* staff was invited to come down and have a drink as a toast to Ann Sheridan.

They held a big luncheon of Warner Bros. executives and stars to witness the turning over of the keys to the truck to Ann Sheridan. Everyone was happy with the wonderful promotion. The stunt got Marty Weiser back to the west coast studio, and he never had to come back to Kansas City.

Psychic detectives John and Mildred Swanson conduct a seance for the press in our living room to contact the spirit of *Agatha* [Christie]

PSYCHIC DETECTIVES

What happened to Agatha Christie during her mysterious disappearance?

Warners was about to release an enthralling mystery called *Agatha*, starring Dustin Hoffman and Vanessa Redgrave. It dealt with Agatha Christie's temporary disappearance during some marital stress many years ago. As a promotional plan, it occurred to us to stage an Agatha seance, and soon we were off and running. In February 1979, we dispatched the following invitation to members of the Kansas City press:

"Everyone loves a mystery ... and you are invited to share one of the most momentous events in the history of the detective story. On Wednesday, February 28th at 7:30 p.m., there is a possibility the late Agatha Christie could reveal the surprise ending to the greatest mystery of her life. Would you like to be a part of that experience?

"Fifty-three years ago Agatha Christie disappeared for eleven days, and the mystery has never been solved. Recent psychic events herald her return from the Other-World to explain the mystery. Noted Kansas City psychics John and Mildred Swanson will conduct a seance in an Old English setting. It is hoped that Dame Agatha, whose own stories reveal her love of the old English country home of "Stiles," will find the English manor conducive to her revelations.

"'The game is afoot,' another famous detective once said. Be there when John and Mildred Swanson assume the roles of psychic detectives to help Dame Agatha reveal the best-kept secret of her life. Your attendance is requested."

The press filled the room, with photographers "hanging over the balcony" for a better view. Leon and Kersti Vitali, assistants to Stanley Kubrick, were also present.

Ours was one of only three promotional seances in the country. Atlanta staged one, and just two weeks before our press seance, another occurred with famed psychic Tamara

Rand in Los Angeles, with the London press in attendance. It brought new information to light: a series of cryptic messages (supposedly from Dame Agatha herself), a mysterious hotel in Constantinople, a hidden key, and a long-lost diary.

Psychics John and Mildred Swanson were optimistic. They had been spiritual consultants in the Kansas City area for many years and had been known for their communication with a fellow Missourian, Mark Twain.

Under the inspiration of Twain, Mildred Swanson had written a psychic book, published in 1968 and was working on another. Her husband, John, was born in Farilla, Sweden, and had originated the Nona board (something like a Ouija Board) which they used the night of the seance. Together they functioned as "psychic detectives" in the tradition of fiction and fact alike, following in the footsteps of Peter Hurkos, Hercule Poirot, John Silence, and Jane Marple.

It wouldn't be the first time a deceased writer has "appeared" to the living to reveal the secrets of an unsolved mystery. Charles Dickens has purportedly appeared numerous times to "solve" his never-finished *The Mystery of Edwin Drood*. Dame Agatha wisely would not allow herself to be outdone by another Brit!

John Swanson, also a trance medium, said before the seance that he had received information "through meditation" about the following:

> "I saw her in England going up rough steps of a stone house that looked very old.

It seemed to be a warm day. The door of the house was open, and Agatha was not wearing a coat. In trying to determine the exact location, which seemed to be near Dover, I saw the letter F and also the letter I."

He believes that the town of Folkstone, near Dover, is where Miss Christie was during the 11 days while a wide search was conducted to find her.

"She apparently stayed with an elderly couple who lived in the house. She needed to get away from the pressures of her career and away from all the people she was in contact with. She just needed a rest."

We wondered how the Swanson's "revelations" would be confirmed during our press event.

The seance was very low-key. The lighting dimmed and soft music played in the background. We made every effort to make it a peaceful setting.

As an introductory part of the seance, the Swansons used the Nona board to hold a conversation with Mark Twain, the famous author of *Tom Sawyer* and *Huckleberry Finn*, by means of sentences spelled out on the board.

The Swansons said they contacted the writer "daily except Sunday."

Mrs. Swanson said: "We believe it is Mark Twain. He says he is Mark Twain, and if he isn't, who is he? Wouldn't it be silly of us to pretend that all of this is happening if it wasn't?"

175

Whatever it was that happened, the Swansons were so positive and confident about their "talking" to Twain that it seemed easy and natural to fall in with the idea.

The Swansons had seen *Agatha* (the film) earlier at an advance press screening. They enjoyed it, especially the photography. They did not like the fictional portrayal of the writer's life because it was not "true-to-life."

In the movie, Miss Christie shows up during her disappearance as having registered under another name in Harrowgate, England, where she shoots pool, plays the piano flamboyantly, and dances the Charleston. All of these are activities that she apparently never engaged in publicly during her lifetime.

When the seance began, we were asked to turn off all the lights except for a "black light."

The audience recited the Lord's Prayer with Mrs. Swanson leading.

She then softly sang several songs during which Mr. Swanson went into a trance.

Four "spirits" spoke through John Swanson: Father Timothy O'Brien, a Roman Catholic priest; Capt. Jonathan Davis, a sea captain; Dr. Andrew Still, the founder of Osteopathy; and Red Cloud, a Shoshoni Indian chief.

The idea was that they would make "contact" with Miss Christie during the seance.

The closest it came was when the Nona Board spelled out "Agatha." Apparently she was present with Twain, and did not like the way she was portrayed in the movie.

The Swansons said they began a week earlier contacting Twain in an attempt to receive some message from Miss Christie.

> "Every day we kept asking Mark, and he would
> keep saying 'there are so many rooms here.'"

It wasn't until just a day or so ago that Twain finally said he had found her.

The seance got a huge front-page break with pictures in the Independence *Examiner* along with coverage from *The Kansan* newspaper, *Boxoffice*—the movie trade magazine along with various radio breaks.

One of the final promotions we did for *Agatha* was on KCMO-AM radio asking listeners to write their versions of what happened to Agatha. The response was outstanding with entries being judged by Mildred Swanson who sent written comments to the winner.

The winner also received a night on the town, including tickets to see the movie *Agatha,* and a private consultation with John Swanson.

Overall, our campaign was a success, and *Agatha* was well-received in the Kansas City area.

TAP CHALLENGE

It was a promotion not to be forgotten, fit for the golden age of movie musicals. Hundreds of tap dancers celebrated the movie *Tap* (1989) that stars Gregory Hines and Sammy Davis, Jr.

The idea for the promotion all started at a Tri-Star publicity meeting in Marina Del Rey, California. Gregory Hines headed the creative meeting with about twenty publicists from Los Angeles, New York, and other cities.

Ideas were brainstormed, and the National Tap Challenge became a reality.

In Kansas City hundreds of onlookers filled Hallmark's Crown Center balconies as costumed tap dancers gathered below.

Mayor Richard L. Berkeley kicked off the event with an official proclamation:

WHEREAS, May 25, 1989, has been designated by a House Joint Resolution as NATIONAL TAP DANCE DAY in honor of Bill "Bojangles" Robinson and in recognition of the important role tap dancing has played and continues to play as the only original American form of dance, and ...

Hundreds of tappers participate in the Kansas City TAP CHALLENGE at Hallmark's Crown Center.

178

WHEREAS, veteran hoofers such as Bunny Briggs, Steve Condos, Arthur Duncan, Harold Nicholas, Sandman Sims, Jimmy Slyde, and Pat Rico put the art form of tap on the map and have watched over the years as its popularity has come and gone, and ...

WHEREAS, the golden age of tap is currently being revitalized through Tri-Star Pictures' National Tap Challenge, the Kansas City Tap Challenge will be held on Saturday, January 14, 1989, at Crown Center, and will produce one local winner who will join thirty-one other winners from the United States and Canada who will compete in Tri-Star Pictures' National Tap Challenge in New York City. The grand-prize winner will receive individual master classes with several tap greats, including Gregory Hines, the star of the new Tri-Star film *Tap*:

NOW, THEREFORE, I, RICHARD L. BERKLEY, Mayor of Kansas City, Missouri, do hereby proclaim Saturday, January 14, 1989, as

KANSAS CITY TAP CHALLENGE DAY

and extend best wishes to the participants in the challenge and commend you for your dedication to this American art form.

Done this 4th day January, 1989, by Richard L.
Berkley - Mayor.

The sounds of tap-dancing rang throughout the Hallmark
Crown Center shops. It was magic to see the costumes
sparkle and glitter and hear the large throng of tappers.

Katey McGuckin, an enthusiastic tapper herself, from
KCPW Radio was MC of the Tap Challenge.

The drama built as Katey enticed a large group of tappers from the audience. As the music started, she led the
warm-up for the challenge.

The big surprise was the extent of audience participation.
Viewers who wanted to tap, but didn't have tap shoes, were
furnished tie-on taps for the dancing. Janis Rovick led the
group activity on the floor.

After the warm-up, the panel of distinguished judges
were introduced:

Lonnie and Ronnie McFadden, Kansas City's
Ambassadors of Dance.
Dr. Doug Moore of WDAF TV 4, NBC.
Betty Valverde (Kaegel).
Louise Renahan (Wilson), Australia.
Jose Espin.
Jodi and Janis Rovick.

Then a truly stunning display of talent unfolded; people
in the audience loved the routines. We had no age limit: tappers ranged from 8 to 33 years old.

Ruby coordinated the Kansas City Tap Challenge, announcing the ten finalists that were selected from more than 70 contestants.

The McFadden Brothers explained the point system the judges used to select the three winners from those top ten:

- 35 possible points for technique—precision of personal style, dancing and ability to execute different steps.
- 35 possible points for stage presence—originality, creativity.
- 30 possible points for enthusiasm—personality used while doing performance.

Judges, Lonnie and Ronnie McFadden discuss the point system with Janis Rovick.

Winner Ashlee Levitch (in center) goes on to dance with Gregory Hines on Broadway. Judges appear in the background. (Photo by Kevin Bertken)

In the end, Kansas City's 12-year-old Ashlee Levitch was number one with the winning balance of technique, stage presence, and personality that the judges were looking for in a tap dancer.

Barry Garron from *The Kansas City Star* reported that she was the winner of the 1989 national tap challenge and that she "danced on Broadway with Gregory Hines."

Later she appeared in commercials for United Telecommunications Inc. and Illinois Bell. In 1991, she appeared in an NBC pilot *I'll Fly Away*.

It was nice to see that our Tap Challenge was one of the touchstones of her success.

As publicists, we won a national prize from Tri-Star Pictures for our work on *Tap*.

How does a publicist create ideas? I reveal my method in the next chapter.

Tibbetts '97

Ray Bradbury
Nov 14, 97

SEVEN

How To Use Your Muse:
and Create Ideas, Magically

Don't think! Thinking is the enemy of creativity. It's self-conscious, and anything self-conscious is lousy. You can't try to do things; you must simply do them.
—*Ray Bradbury*

In Goddess we trust
—Ad tagline, *The Muse*

I dream a lot. I do more painting when I'm not painting. It's in the sub-conscious.
—*Andrew Wyeth*

The imagination must not be given too much material. It must be denied food so that it can work for itself.
—*Macedonlo de la Torre*

An idea can turn to dust or magic, depending on the talent that rubs against it.
—*William Bernbach*, advertising executive

What do you do when inspiration doesn't come: be careful not to spook, get the wind up, or force things into position. You must wait around until the idea comes.
—*John Huston*, film director

RAY BRADBURY, the famous science-fiction writer, told of his life—his transforming encounter at age 12 with Mr. Electrico, a wonderful magician at a carnival who came to visit Waukegan, Illinois.

It was a magical moment for Bradbury to watch Mr. Electrico being electrocuted with his hair standing on end and sparks jumping out of his ears. Then Mr. Electrico put his sword by Bradbury's nose, and electricity shot into his head and out of his ears, and made his hair stand up.

Then Mr. Electrico said: "Live Forever."

Bradbury began his writing career around that time, and never stopped because Mr. Electrico gave him permission to live forever.

It was inspiring to hear Bradbury talk about his experiences over coffee at the Nelson Art Gallery in Kansas City. It showed me the immense power of belief in a magical moment.

The magic of Ray Bradbury's belief strikes at the heart of what movie publicists must generate within themselves and project to others to be successful.

Further, publicists have to believe without question in the idea they present to get cooperation from another person. They must be able to gain willing support through the transfer of their power of belief to those other persons. This permission is similar to how a carnival barker or magician gains believability, referred to as "suspension of disbelief."

Movie and other writers refer to their "Muse." You may have seen the Albert Brooks comedy *The Muse* (1999), starring Sharon Stone. Young women of Greek mythology and legend, according to Socrates, inspired the "divine madness" of the poets. They spurred not only poets and writers, but also all thinkers toward creativity. They visited mortals by night, imparting inspirations and prophecies.

Ray Bradbury's, *Zen in the Art of Writing,* was my first introduction to the concept of "my Muse."

Many writers call it their subconscious. The experience of receiving messages from the subconscious has been described as a subtle form of radar, an inner compass, or a sixth sense. There are several ways the subconscious sends a "phone call":

Through —
- Creative ideas or solutions
- Intuitions
- Inspirations
- Instincts
- Feeling of electricity going through your body
- Uneasy feelings
- Hunches
- Non-rational "Pulls"
- Mental flashes
- Picture or image coming into mind

The following is a six-step formula I use to encourage a visit from my creative Muse. It came from my own publicity experiences in developing ideas and solutions:

C Concentrate on your raw data
R Research your own thinking
E Elaborate on more questions
A Ask for answers
T Trust instead of trying too hard
E Evaluate and refine to reality.

STEP ONE: CONCENTRATE ON YOUR RAW DATA.

In Principle—

Consider this important principle—gather all the information you can. Most of us ignore this principle. It's not as simple as it sounds. Because mental activity follows a pattern, it's hard to break out of everyday responses to become a creative thinker. Ask questions of yourself and others. I use the philosophy that "The only dumb question is the question that is not asked." Define the problem in simple terms: write it down. Use Thoreau's philosophy: simplify … simplify … simplify.

MY METHODS—I organize all the information on 3"x 5" note cards, then break it down into general categories. I use Rudyard Kipling's quote: "I keep six honest serving-men (they taught me all I knew); their names are WHAT and WHY and WHEN and HOW and WHERE and WHO."

Movie composer for *The Sting*, Marvin Hamlisch applies this step, starting with the premise of "what isn't." Throw out everything that is not an elephant; then you're left with what an elephant is.

STEP TWO: RESEARCH YOUR OWN THINKING.

In Principle—

Weave new pathways into your thinking by giving yourself time to digest mentally. You are seeking out new relationships, a synthesis where everything will come together in a neat combination, like a jig-saw puzzle. Watch out for premature judgments or not allowing enough time for your mental digestion to work. A lack of drive can be a block. It's important to believe you are capable of arriving at a creative solution.

MY METHODS—I feel the problem all over with the tentacles of my mind. I take one fact, turn it this way and that way, look at it from different angles, to feel for its true meaning. Then I bring two facts together and see how they fit. I use action verb stimulators. I ADAPT, MODIFY, MAGNIFY, REARRANGE, REVERSE or COMBINE.

As director and writer Robert Benton (*Places in the Heart*) said in a press interview, "When I start writing a new movie script, I have to change my heart." He realizes the value of generating enough emotional motivation to carry him through the new project.

Benton uses a practical working method in his writing. He said, "In considering an actor for a part, I place a picture of him over my typewriter to inspire me about the character for whom I am writing."

Producer Irwin Allen (*Poseidon Adventure*) said in a studio meeting he likes to discuss his production plans with all concerned. He used a three-step process: 1. Writing,

2. Sketches of proposed scenes, and 3. Back to writing to make it work.

STEP THREE: ELABORATE ON MORE QUESTIONS.

In Principle—

When you learn to ask the right questions, you solve many problems, putting you closer to a solution. In step one, you put in writing the answer to "What is the problem?" Now, write down the answer to: "What is the cause of the problem?" Next: "What are the possible solutions?" Last: "Which is the best solution?"

MY METHODS—I ask myself these further questions: "What caused the problem that produced these effects?" "What is similar?" "What contrasts?"

My favorite example from the movies is Stanley Kubrick who had his assistants seek answers to minute details and report to him. This way, Kubrick was able to capture detailed reality in such movies as *2001:A Space Odyssey* (1968).

STEP FOUR: ASK FOR ANSWERS.

In *Principle—*

You will tend to achieve what you think you can achieve because it creates a path in the mind for a solution. Timing is important when seeking creative answers. The best time is when the emotions are calm. You need time to think so that the subconscious has a chance to be heard.

MY METHODS—I quietly ask my subconscious for a "solution." Sometimes, I use the word "solution" several times throughout the day until an answer comes. I may repeat a statement like this: "There is a perfect solution to this problem and that answer is being sent through my subconscious mind."

As Clint Eastwood told Barbara Walters on ABC in 1982:

> "There's a little guy right inside the back (of my head) there, and he says 'Don't do that.' … I feel where I've gone today has been mostly based on instinct, animal instinct."

Quincy Jones suggests, "Dream—Pray—Listen to your instincts."

STEP FIVE: TRUST INSTEAD OF TRYING TOO HARD.

In *Principle*—
You need to relax your body and mind before ideas will flow. Some of us become so overwhelmed by a problem that we end up with fear or a "frozen up" response. Tension slows down, or even stops the creation of ideas.

MY METHODS—I empty my mind with the 3 R's: I relax, rely, and release. I get involved in other activities and let the ideas come on their own.

Film director John Schlesinger said, "You can't explain or analyze some fears. It's something you feel inside you, like a hunch or intuition. It's uniquely your own. So when you experience a feeling you can't account for, stop and ask yourself, why? Why do I feel this way?"

Actor Mel Gibson places great trust in his skill. Gibson told to the *Christian Science Monitor* when playing *Hamlet,* "I had to go for my gut instincts on how to play the role. I've learned you can't let someone directly tell you what to do. At these times you have to trust your intuition. That was the best way I was able to get myself into character."

STEP SIX: EVALUATE AND REFINE TO REALITY.

In *Principle—*

You might not test the idea to reality because of objections of others or objections coming from inside yourself. Some think of all sorts of excuses why something won't work. Many experts warn not to talk over your ideas too much with others who might be critical.

Another block is the need for perfection. Creative individuals fear making a mistake that might embarrass them in the eyes of others. You may have to balance becoming more successful with new ideas, against the approval of others. Ask yourself "What is in my own best interest?"

MY METHODS—To refine my idea or solution to reality, I use the KISS formula: I keep it simple and sweet. When you see something as big, you can still keep it simple. I ask myself: Do people get it? Does it explode in their minds? I use the following philosophy: "All things considered, the simplest answer is the best."

Director Roman Polanski said to Charlie Rose on movie making, "I concentrate daily on my first vision of a movie. I see how it relates to the new reality that superimposes itself on my imagined movie."

In conclusion, here are a few methods I use until my Muse comes so that I feel I'm taking action:

● If I ordinarily type out my notes, I write them in my own handwriting instead.

- I change my environment. I walk into a different book store I've never been in. There I encounter things I've never seen. This change stimulates my brain.
- I change my lunch habits. I eat where ordinarily I don't, and since I normally eat *with* someone, I'll eat alone.
- Or I find a way to drop the problem. I do something that stimulates my imagination and emotions.

Creative ideas are power tools in Hollywood. Next, learn seven of their secrets and how to use them.

Ruby, between Alan Alda and Christopher Reeve at
the Show-A-Rama "Dinner with the Stars" in 1979.

EIGHT

Seven Hollywood Success Strategies...*and how to use them*

Best Movie Star...Julia Roberts—*Time* magazine (2001)

Why let two thousand years of publicity go to waste?
—*Cecil B. DeMille*, explaining why he was remaking *The Ten Commandments* (1956)

How much does it cost me if it's free?
—*Colonel Tom Parker*, agent for Elvis Presley

The most important word in the vocabulary of advertising is TEST. If you pretest your product with consumers, and pretest your advertising, you will do well in the marketplace.
—*David Ogilvy*, advertising executive

The postman wants an autograph. The cab driver wants a picture. The waitress wants a handshake. Everyone wants a piece of you.
—*John Lennon*

We are the only company whose assets all walk out the gate at night.
—*Louis B. Mayer*, MGM

THE PURSUIT OF POWER is the basic nature of the Hollywood studios. Making, distributing, and publicizing movies are full of struggles for power. Hollywood agent Larry Thompson says would-be stars begin by wanting only fame, but then they want power.

The practice is to get others to do what one wants; the lever is the power of authority. Power is the motivation on all levels from stars to the studio bosses.

Annually, *Premiere* magazine publishes its "Top 100 Hollywood Power Players." Based on these lists, publicity becomes the driving power behind the star and the box-office appeal of their movies. It lists in straight-forward manner how the players rank, last year's ranking, pending projects, and what their strengths and weaknesses offer. The top-grossing films are reported continually in the *Hollywood Reporter* and *Daily Variety*. These sources keep the score on power in Hollywood.

Publicity's impact on perception in Hollywood may be more important than reality in Hollywood, because perception translates into power. A widely-known star once said, "There are many stars, but few great actors." Tom Hanks has proved himself a great actor and has been acclaimed by his Hollywood peers with the honor of three Best Actor® Academy Awards. This credibility gives Tom Hanks considerable power. Julia Roberts, as critic Emanuel Levy says, "… represents everything Hollywood loves—glamour, talent, power."

Then there is the power of the screen itself: the power to stimulate audiences, inspire images upon the media, and impress the public to favor a particular movie or leading star.

The following are seven time-tested ways Hollywood manufactures publicity power and how to use them.

1. GET INTO THE HABIT OF TESTING. You can make testing work, even if you cannot do costly test marketing.

Movies are generally multi-million-dollar investments; therefore, the demand from the studio heads is that every aspect of a movie be measured. Hollywood has to build information into an effective marketing strategy, so the movie will appeal to the largest possible audience.

For example, on the Chevy Chase comedy, *Funny Farm*, the first thing I did was review what had been proven successful on two earlier comedies, *National Lampoon's Vacation* and *Blazing Saddles*. I took the elements that worked and incorporated them into the *Funny Farm* promotion. On-line or library research is one way you can find information inexpensively.

Studios use exhibitor screenings to get advance response from theater owners before they are released.

Another tool is inexpensive surveys, and even small samples are better than none at all. Audience-reaction studies work well in theatres and even in shopping centers.

Research may show that a movie released as a PG-13 will attract more movie-goers than a PG. In essence, Hollywood functions to give the public what it wants.

Another way to monitor the pulse of an audience is to do on-location-theatre-exit interviews just after a movie has ended while images are still fresh. Individual viewers can be a great source as listening posts for information. Depending on the theme of the movie, I would invite individuals to attend showings and report reactions. We used demographic reports that broke down information, such as the age groups and sex of members of an audience.

How often do you sit in a theatre and watch trailers of upcoming movies, sometimes months before they are released? Pre-testing the reaction to a movie is a common studio device to predict its appeal. Today, strong Internet interest in a trailer can tip off a studio that a film might develop a following. This approach seems to work best for movies that draw younger audiences. Testing is essential.

2. BUILD YOUR OWN THINK TANK. Two or three individuals can join to make a think tank with the common purpose of creating new ideas.

I've found a certain creative flow can be generated through discussing ideas with others. This technique was invaluable at major studio publicity meetings and was developed to an art form.

Imagine the mind power and experience of publicists from twenty or more major cities coming together to brainstorm. From all the suggested ideas, the most promising were compiled, edited by studio publicists, and examined by individual publicists for potential use in their regions.

The brainstorming technique gave way to more and more creativity, often with the director, producer, or the star active in some aspect of the meeting.

Another technique I've found productive is to work on several creative projects at the same time because ideas hitch-hike on one another. You may create an idea on one campaign that fits just as well on an unrelated campaign.

3. LOOK FOR THE "BIG IDEA" which will likely become the theme of your campaign. Always ask yourself: "Can this local promotion be extended to reach regionally or nationally?" Keep in mind it is better to do one coordinated promotion that fits and ties into your "Big Idea" than to use unrelated ideas that take-away from the theme.

On the movie *The Swarm,* it took only a few minutes for Ruby to create the new Disco Dance "The Swarm," which played up the tongue-in-cheek humor instead of the terror surrounding the movie.

4. YOUR CONTACTS HAVE CONTACTS. You may not know how to get publicity or a promotion done directly, but you probably know someone whose influence can help.

Ask yourself, "Do I know any particular person who could positively influence the acceptance of my idea?"

In life as in Hollywood, you need a firm footing and the courage to persevere.

In Hollywood, things don't just happen. It takes a concerted effort to position a movie through advance publicity.

Studios use this principle to build word-of-mouth publicity before to the release of many new movies.

Sony went after influential viewers with early screenings of *Crouching Tiger, Hidden Dragon (2000)* starring Michelle Yeoh and Chow Yun-Fat, to make it a "cross over" movie to gain a broader audience. Without such a ploy, the film might be just a another karate or art film. Sony set a screening for women, hosted by *Sports Illustrated* magazine. The idea was to create word-of-mouth with a core group of female athletes.

When Russell Crowe was to be on the cover of *Talk* magazine, Dreamworks and *Talk* sponsored a screening for 150 special invitees to see *Gladiator* (2000) at New York's Ziegfeld Theater, followed by a dinner at restaurant Circo. Gossip columnist, Liz Smith, ran a follow-up article.

5. ALWAYS HAVE A BACK-UP PLAN. When you have a special event, have a fall-back alternative. It might be to invite an extra 20 percent to assure a good turn-out. Or it might be as simple a thing as to consider, when planning an outdoor event, what you will do if it rains.

Warner Bros. sent Dr. Nancy Thomas, a renowned Egyptologist to Kansas City to promote *The Sphinx* (1981). She had been a consultant on the production of the film itself. (Nancy is the daughter of the famed Hollywood columnist, Bob Thomas).

Dr. Thomas was scheduled to hold a press conference before a live audience at a premiere showing. It was already in progress before her flight landed in Kansas City. Then we discovered her flight was delayed. Ruby initiated a back-up plan to keep an audience of 400, including film critics, involved in a question-and-answer session until Dr. Thomas arrived at the theatre.

She walked into an immediate introduction just as the last question had been announced.

The back-up plan saved the press conference.

Later Dr. Thomas made an interesting point about the back-up plans of the Egyptians:

"When they were not in the fields, they were in the military, building pyramids. They had a back-up plan for every one of their activities."

6. ASK YOURSELF: "HOW MUCH DOES IT COST ME IF IT'S FREE?" That question was continually asked by Elvis Presley's agent, Colonel Tom Parker, when it came to the exposure of Elvis. Colonel Parker protected the value of Elvis by guarding against over-exposure or the wrong type of exposure. He wanted to make sure the public continued to pay for the privilege of seeing Elvis.

No other agent has been as successful as Parker at protecting the publicity value of a star since the time of Louis B. Mayer at MGM. Under Mayer's reign, big names such as Clark Gable did not make TV appearances so that their boxoffice appeal would remain strong. If fans wanted to see their favorite star, they would have to go to a theatre. Over-exposure can mean less money potential for a star.

I have found that the public's value of a promotion is based on what they will pay for it. What is meant by "pay" is not just money. Rather, what creative effort does the public have to put out to earn something? The more energy the public puts into responding to a promotion, the more potential the promotion has. For example, an art contest could require creative involvement, or a radio station might have listeners call in to answer questions.

7. USE THE POWER OF CELEBRITY ENDORSE-MENTS.

If the Nike shoe company says its shoes are the best, everyone knows its purpose is to sell shoes.

But if Tiger Woods says Nike Shoes are the best and wears them ...

If Roger Ebert—or your local critic—recommends a movie ...

If Isabella Rossellini endorses a certain brand of perfume ... then the public "knows" the product is good because the endorsement comes from someone held in high esteem.

It's the same in any town, city, or region the publicist serves. Quotes, recommendations, or endorsements from respected public figures usually do more for a film than any agency-generated advertisement copy. Generated publicity (which is usually free while advertising is paid for) are testimonials that are hard to beat, along with other kinds of endorsements.

The positive quotes are passed on to the studio advertising department, and some end up in the newspaper advertising campaign. Movie ad quotes, such as "Best Picture of the Year," or "One of the Year's Ten Best," become great testimonials that cannot be bought.

Publicity photos are effective when the picture tells a story and has a visual element of surprise. Be sure to carry visuals such as stills and posters at all publicity events, and even have a camera on hand in case some unique opportunity might arise.

I estimate that free publicity space or broadcast time is worth three times as much as equivalent advertising would cost. If a 60 second TV spot would cost $1,000, then a 60-second free publicity break would be worth $3,000. As you can tell, publicity adds a lot of increased value to the movies from Hollywood's viewpoint.

After your campaign is ended, it is important to evaluate the dollar value of the exposure you received. Or if increased sales were your target—did you reach your goal?

What did you learn? How will it help you in your next campaign?

In the end,
everything
is a gag
—*Charles Chaplin*

NINE

A Parting Shot

LOOKING BACK, I FEEL FORTUNATE to have worked with some of the Hollywood greats. The past experiences act as a platform to help shape movie publicity in the future.

Today's publicist is moving into a wider electronic media. Movie marketers now seek an interactive relationship with film fans. For example, digital technology would allow direct delivery of movie selections to theatres or individual households. However, many feel that seeing a first-run film in a theatre with an audience will remain the preferred way to see a movie.

As George Lucas said about future filmmakers and the coming digital-cinema in *USA Today*,

> "I think we are in the arena now that's similar to the advent of sound and color. Now it's a matter of how creative artists [including publicists] use these new realms."

With future technology shifts, the non-traditional definition of Hollywood will become more relevant:

> It's a place of escape, where you fulfill the drama needed in your daily life.

Chaplin leaves Kansas City (1913), following vandeville stints in New York and across the country to start his movie career in Hollywood. His last stage performance with the Karno Company was at the Empress Theater, 12th and McGee, Kansas City, Missouri.

Hollywood will be wherever you are. The movie experience will become a more immediate personal experience, available in more and more ways and places.

Often, I think back to the conversation I had with Ben Shlyen, the founder of *Boxoffice* trade magazine.

Ben said to me,

> "The best things that happen to the movie business are never planned; they come out of left field."

Many creative ideas also come out of left field. So you can bet when changes come, there will be publicists nearby working their magic to help stars and their movies find their future.

Notes

**Chapter 1: HOW I FOUND THE TRUE HOLLYWOOD:
AN INSIDER'S UNCONVENTIONAL VIEW**

Page 1 Dictionary definitions from *Peter's Quotations*, *The Penguin Dictionary of Humorous Quotations*, *Simpson's Contemporary Quotations* and *Film Quotations*

Page 4 William Saroyan quote from David Pirie, *Anatomy of the Movies*, Macmillian, 1981

Page 4 Armond Aserinsky quote to Rick Lyman, *New York Times*, March 12, 2001

Page 7 William Goldman as quoted by Peter Hay from *When the Lion Roars*

Page 9 Russell Crowe quote, Chris Vognar, *The Dallas Morning News*, April 1, 2001

Page 12 James Ellroy quote to Robert Butler, *The Kansas City Star*, September 14, 1997

Page 17 Mayo interview questions on Ronald Reagan by Kevin Minton, *Classic Images*, January, 1995

Chapter 2: HOW PUBLICISTS ADD A MAGIC OF THEIR OWN

Page 21 Dictionary definitions from *The Quotable Quote Book*, *American Heritage Dictionary of Quotations*, and *20,000 Quips and Quotes*

Page 21 Humphrey Bogart quote from Candice Fuhrman, *Publicity Stunt!*, Chronicle Books, 1989

Page 21 Jack Warner quote from Lester Gordon, *Let's Go to the Movies!*, Santa Monica Press, 1992

Page 22 William Goldman, *Adventures in the Screen Trade*, Warner Books, 1983

Page 23 David Puttnam, *Movies and Money*, Alfred A. Knopf, 1998

Page 24 Julius Epstein quote by Algean Harmetz, *New York Times,* January 1, 2001

Page 33 Connie Bruck, *The New Yorker*, August 13, 2001

Chapter 3: WAYS PUBLICISTS CREATE STAR POWER

Page 41 Dictionary quotes from the *Penguin Thesaurus of Quotations* and *Film Quotations* and *Oxford Dictionary of 20ᵗʰ Century Quotations*

Page 41 Hugh Grant to Julia Roberts quoted from *Notting Hill* review, *New York Times*, May 28, 1999

Page 41 Russell Crowe quote, Robert Butler, *The Kansas City Star*, October 5, 1997

Page 41 Woody Allen quote from David Pirie, *Anatomy of the Movies*, MacMillan, 1981

Page 48 Junket definition by Ty Burr with Steve Daly, *Entertainment Weekly*, July 20, 2001

Page 48 Dana Kennedy and Terry Press quotes from "Where a nose for news may be out of joint," by Dana Kennedy, *The New York Times*, May 13, 2001

BEHIND-THE-SCENES STORIES WITH CELEBRITIES

ERNEST BORGNINE

Page 53 Borgnine quote from *Film Quotations*

BUSTER CRABBE

Page 57 *Films in Review*, July - August, 1996

Page 57 *Kansas City Times*, April 8, 1977

Page 58 *Boxoffice*, April 18, 1977

MARK HARMON

Page 69 Mark Harmon as quoted by Robert C. Trussell, *The Kansas City Times*, April 27, 1979

ICE-T

Pages 73-75 *New Jack City* press conference for Ice-T, February 19, 1991 in Kansas City

Page 73 Ice-T quotes to Ward Triplett III, *The Kansas City Star*, March 8, 1991

CHUCK JONES (ANIMATOR / DIRECTOR)

Pages 77-78 National press conference held in Kansas City with Chuck Jones in 1990, portions aired on Time Warner Cable, on June 3, 1990

Pages 78-79 Fritz Freleng, Kansas City press conference, 1990

STANLEY KUBRICK

Page 80 Marlon Brando quote from Joanne Stang, *The New York Times Magazine* October 12, 1958

Pages 83-84 Lee Ermey article by Robert W. Butler, *The Kansas City Star,* July 28, 1987

RUSH LIMBAUGH (A.K.A. JEFF CHRISTIE)

Pages 86-90 *Heroes of All-Time* (1993), aired on Time Warner Cable

GEORGE MILLER (*MAD MAX II* DIRECTOR)

Pages 92-94 George Miller quotes from David Chute, *Film Comment*, July-August 1982

Pages 92-94 George Miller quoted by Robert W. Butler, *The Kansas City Star*, July 29, 1982

Notes

MICHAEL MOORE (*ROGER & ME*)
Page 97 Michael Moore quote from *Internet Movie Database*
PEGGY REA
Pages 101-102 Peggy Rea quotes, Robert W. Butler, *The Kansas City Star,* September 29, 1989
CHRISTOPHER REEVE
Page 105 American Classic Screen, March - April 1979
Pages 106-107 Christopher Reeve as quoted by Shifra Stein, *The Kansas City Times,* April 27, 1979
STEVEN SEAGAL
Pages 108-109 Seagal quotes from press conference, March 21, 1988
JOHN TRAVOLTA
Page 112 Travolta quote from *Playboy* magazine
DEE WALLACE (STONE)
Pages 117-118 Dee Wallace quote by Kathy Mackay, *People's Weekly*, December 6, 1982
Page 118 "At the Movies," Chris Chase, *The New York Times,* August 26, 1983
JACK L. WARNER (THE LAST MOGUL)
Page 119 Jack Warner quote about Bette Davis from *Simpson's Contemporary Quotations*
Page 119 Bette Davis quote about Jack Warner, *Variety* magazine, September 13, 1978
Page 120 David Puttnam, *Movies and Money*, Alfred A. Knopf, 1998
FOREST WHITAKER (*BIRD*, 1988)
Page 125 Eastwood quote about Parker to Richard Schickel, *Clint Eastwood*, Alfred Knopf, 1996

Chapter 4: HOW THE MOVIE PEOPLE DO GOOD WORKS
Page 131 Dictionary definitions from *The Quotable Quote Book* and *Film Quotations*
Page 131 Zuzu's Wonderful Life in the Movies by Christopher Brunell, orders to Wonderful Life Studios, P. O. Box 145, Carnation, WA 98014
Pages 137-139 NBC interview, December 23, 1994, *It's a Wonderful Life* with Karolyn Grimes (ZuZu).
Chapter 5: HOW HUMOR ENTICES YOU TO THE BOX OFFICE
Page 141 Dictionary quotes from *The Quotable Quote Book* and *The Dictionary of Film Quotations*
Pages 144, 149-151 Marty Weiser taped interview, 1987

209

Page 149 "Virginia Mayo in Mishap; She Loses (?) Swim Suit," P. 1, *Denver Post*, July 7, 1949

Page 150 "Mayo 'Top Undressed Woman," say Nudists Page 1, "Nudists Like Mayo Photo," Page 2, *Denver Post*, August 18, 1949

Chapter 6: HOW DRAMA DRAWS YOU TO THE MOVIES

Page 159 Alfred Hitchhock quote from *Redbook*, April, 1963

Pages 163-164 Psycho ad copy from *Those Great Movie Ads*, 1972, Galahad Books

Pages 164-167 Diabolique Exhibitor's Manual

Page 169-171 Marty Weiser taped interview, 1987

Pages 174-176 Charles Burke, *Examiner*, March 3, 1979

Chapter 7: HOW TO USE YOUR MUSE

Page 185 Dictionary quotes from *The Quotable Quote Book* and *Simpson's Contemporary Quotations*

Page 187 Ray Bradbury, *Zen in the Art of Writing*, Capra Press, 1990

Pages 188-190 James Webb Young, *A Technique for Producing Ideas*, Advertising Publications, Inc., 1965

Page 188 Hamlisch quote to Larry King on *CNN*, March 19, 1986

Page 191 Clint Eastwood quote to Richard Schickel, *Clint Eastwood*, Alfred A. Knopf, 1996

Page 192 Roman Polanski quote to Charlie Rose, *PBS*, March 9, 2000

Chapter 8: SEVEN HOLLYWOOD SUCCESS STRATEGIES

Page 195 Dictionary quotes from *Simpson's Contemporary Quotations* and *Let's Go to the Movies!* by Gordon

Page 196 Breaking Through, Selling Out, Dropping Dead by William Bayer, The Macmillan Company, 1971

Page 200 John Lippman quotes on *Crouching Tiger* and *Gladiator*, *The Wall Street Journal*, January 11, 2001

Chapter 9: A PARTING SHOT

Page 204 The Quotable Quote Book

Page 205 Lucas quote from Marco R. della Cava, *USA Today*, February 23, 2001

Painting and Photo Credits

To the many photographers, librarians and others who aided in my efforts to illustrate this book, "Thank You." The author particularly expresses gratitude to Dr. John Tibbetts for the original paintings used throughout the book. The paintings and publicity photos are from the author's personal collection, except as noted here.

Courtesy of *American Classic Screen*, 56,104, 204

Courtesy of *Boxoffice* magazine, 58, 168

Karolyn Grimes and Christopher Brunell, 130

Courtesy of *The Kansan*, Kansas City, Ks, 116

Special Collections, Kansas City Missouri Public Library, 140

Courtesy of *The Kansas City Star and Times*, 127

Museum of Modern Art, New York, 57 © Warner Bros. 80, 92, 119

Courtesy of Show-A-Rama, 68, 106, 112, 194

Dr. John Tibbetts, x, 14, 16, 20, 56, 60, 104, 184

Courtesy of United Motion Picture Organization, 158

Courtesy of Universal Pictures, 63

Courtesy of Warner Bros., 121, 159

Courtesy of WDAF-TV, 42, 43, 50, 101

Name Index